28.6.79.

The Geography of
Laws and Justice

Keith D. Harries
Stanley D. Brunn

The Geography of Laws and Justice

Spatial Perspectives on the Criminal Justice System

Praeger Publishers   New York   London

Library of Congress Cataloging in Publication Data

Harries, Keith D
    The geography of laws and justice.

    Includes bibliographical references.
    1. Criminal justice, Administration of—United
States. I. Brunn, Stanley D., joint author.
    II. Title
HV8138.H37   364'.973   77-25460
ISBN 0-03-022331-8

PRAEGER SPECIAL STUDIES
200 Park Avenue, New York, N.Y., 10017, U.S.A.

Published in the United States of America in 1978
by Praeger Publishers,
A Division of Holt, Rinehart and Winston, CBS, Inc.

89   038   987654321

Printed in the United States of America

For those who suffer spatial injustice

ACKNOWLEDGMENTS

Many individuals have contributed in some way to the preparation of this book. At Oklahoma State University, the Cartography Service of the Department of Geography, directed by Don Wade and with the assistance of Gayle Maxwell, did excellent work. Linda Allred and Marcia Hickman somehow typed manuscript in the midst of a thousand other chores. Linda, the scholarly secretary, always managed to meet deadlines somehow, in spite of the pressures of her job and her Ph.D. program. Graduate assistants Gary Lauver, Mike Johnson, and Cindy Quinlan suffered through the verification of a large data set. Programmer Judy Henry kept her sanity through circumstances bizarre enough to be ludicrous. Russ Lura, currently a Ph.D. student at Syracuse University, is thanked for his work on federal sentencing--originally a masters degree research paper--contained in Chapter 6. John Rooney and Dick Hecock, as Chairman and Acting Chairman, respectively, of the Department of Geography are thanked for encouraging faculty creativity; they and other colleagues provided invaluable support during periods of therapeutic time-wasting.

At Michigan State University, Emily Palmer and Kit Stapler typed manuscript and their work is much appreciated. Professor Lawrence Sommers, Chairman of the Department of Geography, and Dean Gwen Andrew of the College of Social Science, are thanked for the provision of release teaching time for work on the manuscript. Assistance was also provided through a Michigan State University All-University Research Grant.

Several publishers and authors have kindly granted permission for the use or adaptation of their copyrighted works: Henry Robert Glick, "The System of State and Local Courts," Current History 60 (1971), including selections from pp. 342, 346, and 347; the Pennsylvania Geographer approved the use of a figure that appeared on p. 29 of vol. 13, no. 1. The American Judicature Society allowed the adaptation of "The Geography of Justice: Sentencing Variations in U.S. Judicial Districts," Judicature 57 (1974), pp. 392-401. Harper and Row, Publishers, granted permission for the adaptation of maps appearing in Daniel J. Elazar, American Federalism: A View from the States (second edition), originally published by Thomas Crowell in 1972. The adapted maps appeared on pp. 106-07 and 110-11.

In spite of the patience and assistance of the persons mentioned above, and the same qualities in the Praeger editorial and production staffs, there are inevitable errors and omissions for which the authors accept full responsibility.

CONTENTS

LIST OF TABLES

LIST OF MAPS AND FIGURE

The Geography of
Laws and Justice

The last decade has been a period of crisis for the U.S. criminal justice system. Attention has been focused on enormous abuses of the system, ranging from police brutality to unequal justice and devastating prison disturbances. Beneath the hyperbole, there have been nagging and perplexing dilemmas. Could the rising crime rate be curbed? Do more police mean less crime? Should court autonomy be challenged or modified? Could inequities in sentencing be eliminated? Should the apparently ineffectual concept of rehabilitation be abandoned? Definitive answers to these questions may never emerge, but the period of crisis has had at least one constructive outcome: Assumptions about the structure and operation of criminal justice institutions have been challenged with increasing frequency, and many have fallen, to be replaced by improved knowledge--new principles better able to withstand rigorous scientific tests, or tests of use and experience. Other monuments to tradition, such as police patrol, are leaning precariously on their pedestals and are the subject of continuing and often acrimonious debate among lay people and specialists.

In this context of the reexamination of institutions, methods, and values within criminal justice, the laws and the courts have resisted change as effectively as any other system element. The blatant inequities surrounding place-to-place variations in laws, jury selection methods, and defendant processing have been exemplified on an almost daily basis.

It has become patently obvious that the place in which criminal events or civil litigation occur may have a profound influence on outcomes. In some cases, where an event occurs may determine whether a citizen is judged a felon, a misdemeanant, or not guilty of committing a crime, in the sense that acts considered legal in some jurisdictions are illegal in others. In such circumstances, the concept of morality, or what is right behavior from a societal point of view, takes on a regional or local dimension. Such a regional dimension may have been appropriate in a frontier society of limited mobility, but today's foot-loose citizens, migrating at will in response to job opportunities or perceptions of quality of life, are often disoriented and perplexed by the realization that seemingly innocuous behavior-- such as consuming liquor by the drink or betting on horses or dogs-- may be felonious. One may have less sympathy for the burglar who complains that sentences are longer in state A than in state B, but, sympathetic or not, we should inquire about the purpose and effectiveness of such variations, and challenge them if they have no other reason for existing than to proclaim the sovereignty of states.

Why are geographers interested in phenomena related to justice? Geographers have always been fascinated by the phenomenon of place-- the chemistry of attitudes, environment, and happenstance that distinguishes one place from another. Traditionally, a great deal of emphasis has been placed by geographers on economic explanations of regional variations in phenomena, an emphasis attributed by Fraser Hart to the middle western bias in the production of geographers. This bias, suggested Hart, has meant that numerous professional geographers have seen the world through a filter of middle western values, two of which he labeled "pecuniaristic" and "materialistic."[1] Such economic emphasis has been fading rapidly in the last decade, and few would seek today to interpret spatial variations in complex social geography through economic factors alone. This is certainly true when one looks at the criminal justice system. While the more affluent states tend to be progressive in criminal justice matters, they continue to be riddled with problems--the economic might of the state of New York helped "produce" the 1971 Attica prison riots; at the same time, the relatively humble state of Oklahoma spawned the devastating 1973 riot at "Big Mac," the state penitentiary at McAlester. Primitive red-necked sheriffs are usually associated with the rural South, while metropolitan Washington, D.C. was the source of intrigue, during the Watergate period, that made the congeries of uncovered crimes landmarks in American history, particularly when the differential treatment of the various offenders is taken into account. Observation of the actions of the criminal justice system leads to the suspicion that it is in reality a nonsystem. It is, rather, a series of open systems pretending to mesh together--but failing--and the end product is near anarchy.

The glare of publicity has fallen frequently upon law enforcement and corrections. The former has enjoyed rising budgets as a response to public fear of crime, while being damned for failing to solve the problem. Corrections departments have been blamed for letting offenders out too early, for failing to rehabilitate, for allowing escapes, and for escalating costs. The judicial process has managed to come through relatively unscathed, a tribute to the autocracy of the judiciary and the reticence of prosecutors. The judiciary has guarded its secrets so well that few observers have been able to fathom whether it has done a good job or not. Even now, with the cat out of the bag, so to speak, few prosecutors or judges, like college professors, are ever the subject of disciplinary proceedings for ineptitude, incompetence, or corruption. Judges, in particular, are essentially untouchable unless their conduct is so bizarre that it threatens to embarrass the whole judiciary.

It is against this backdrop of legal-judicial problems that this volume has been prepared. The authors, through convergent research primarily in political and social geography, have developed an appreciation for, and a concern about, the blatant inequities and inefficiencies present in the judicial process. This concern is expressed here by using a geographic perspective--a preoccupation with the impact of boundaries, of territorial laws and judicial systems, and of differential prosecutorial or judicial actions between jurisdictions. This book is intended to be a consciousness raiser rather than a problem solver. But policy makers and technicians involved in the problem-solving process may find virtues in the geographic perspective presented here.

Virtually every problem of the legal-judicial system has a spatial component, often implying inequity as a result of historical inertia, ignorance and disinterest, or intentional manipulation. The National Advisory Commission on Criminal Justice Standards and Goals, in its 358-page document, Courts, set down a list of problems and proposed solutions, some of which are touched upon later in this book. One illustrative example is the issue of delay in the disposition of cases. The commission noted that in many states, statutes prescribe maximum periods for stages of felony prosecutions, ranging from 75 days to six months.[2] Here is a clear example of potentially differential treatment between states. But within states, another basis for unequal treatment exists in the differences between district courts. Some districts are efficient and keep cases moving as rapidly as possible; in others, crowded calendars, possibly combined with managerial ineptitude or inadequate administrative resources, mean long delays in processing. These delays, of course, can make a mockery of the principle of a person being innocent until proven guilty, when defendants are incarcerated for unreasonable periods prior to trial.

When spatial variations in laws, law enforcement efficiency, prosecutor toughness, jail and prison conditions, disposition time for cases, judicial competence, jury role and selection processes, and the effectiveness of probation and parole systems are considered, one can begin to develop an appreciation for the role of what may be loosely called place in the judicial process.

An additional, and dramatic brief example of the impact of spatial differences in laws and justice may be developed in connection with regional variations in the application of the death penalty. If justice is being dispensed evenly, and with other things being equal, we would expect that the regional shares of the total number of persons under sentence of death would crudely approximate the regional shares of homicides reported. But when the data are examined, they reveal substantial differences in shares--in fact, not even the regional rank orders of death-row residents and of homicides match (see Table 1.1). The lowest regional share of homicides was recorded in the West (16.7 percent), but the lowest proportion on death row was found in the Northeast (1.1 percent). The South, long notorious for its high rates of both homicide and execution, had 42.2 percent of the homicides, but 75.2 percent of the death-row inmates. If the data are broken down further, it is found that in December 1976 Florida had the most prisoners on death row (81)--some 17 percent of the national total. Yet Florida had only 6 percent of the national homicides. In all, Florida, California (68), and Ohio (67) accounted for 46 percent of those under sentence of death, while reporting only 21 percent of all homicides.

TABLE 1.1

Regional Comparisons of Homicides Versus Prisoners
under Death Sentence, 1975

Region	State Prisoners under Sentence of Death[a]		Reported Homicides and Nonnegligent Manslaughters	
	Number	Percent of National Total	Number	Percent of National Total
Northeast	5	1.1	3,758	18.3
North Central	42	8.9	4,663	22.7
South	355	75.2	8,660	42.2
West	70	14.8	3,424	16.7
Total	472	100.0	20,505	99.9[b]

[a]On December 31, 1975.
[b]Rounding error.
Sources: Federal Bureau of Investigation, Uniform Crime Reports (Washington, D.C.: U.S. Government Printing Office, 1976), Table 3, pp. 50-55; U.S. Department of Justice, Capital Punishment 1976, Advance Report (Washington, D.C.: U.S. Department of Justice, April 1977).

As the reader knows, other things are in fact far from equal, creating extraordinary differences between states in the probability of the death sentences. Several states (Maine, Michigan, Wisconsin, Minnesota, Iowa, West Virginia, Oregon, Alaska, and Hawaii) either have historically had no capital punishment or have abolished it. The constitutionality of the death penalty in various states has been challenged, and North Carolina's death-row population declined from 103 to zero between December 1975 and December 1976 as a result of one ruling. In 1977, in the case of white Georgia rapist Erlich Coker, the U.S. Supreme Court ruled that the death penalty was "grossly disproportionate and excessive punishment for the crime of rape," thus removing six rapists from death rows across the country. Historically, capital punishment for rape had been used (principally in the South) primarily on black men who had raped white women (405 of the 455 executed for rape since 1930 were black).[3] Various facets of capital punishment are still under scrutiny in the U.S. Supreme Court, and it is likely that other state statutes will be rejected or modified in the future. Whatever subsequent changes occur, it is clear that homicides committed under similar conditions by similar kinds of people will continue to attract the death penalty in some states, but not in others. An observer from another planet might come to the conclusion that homicide is considered a more wicked act on one side of a state boundary than on the other. (Some additional comments on the geography of capital punishment are made in Chapter 6.)

The capital punishment example is striking since it has, at least potentially, a direct bearing on the termination of human life. Most of the issues dealt with in this book are much less impelling, at least individually, but when considered cumulatively they alter the courses of many individuals' lives, often in traumatic and inequitable ways. Our selection of topics is admittedly limited, and tends to focus on questions that we have found ourselves concerned about in recent years.

In Chapter 2, attention is drawn to some of the spatial impacts of interjurisdictional variations in statutes. The variation that exists is presented within the context of contrasting regional social philosophies. The crosscurrents of migration that have moved across the nation in varying directions and magnitude in the past several centuries have been responsible for regional philosophies emerging and have influenced the types of statutes enacted. Various groups settled in different regions, and their views on individual rights, acceptable social behaviors, and government responsibility are behind the differences in statutes, and in their interpretation, that exist today. A number of specific contrasts are examined at local and state levels to illustrate how tradition and regional philosophy have evolved and help explain the present geography of statutes.

Jury selection may not seem at first glance to have significant geographical connotations, yet jury selection methods and requests for changes in the venue of trials, predicated upon changed juror response at the new location, are two clearly spatially related variables as discussed in Chapter 3. The ability of social scientists to predict jury decisions (within limits), based on the socioeconomic characteristics of jurors, forces analysis of population attributes that are extremely specific to locale. In Chapter 3, several examples of jury manipulation are reviewed, and the possible role of geographers in jury selection and analysis is discussed with the aid of hypothetical examples.

A critical issue that has come increasingly to the fore is variation in sentencing. Chapters 4, 5, and 6 relate to this problem. The importance of unjustified disparities in sentencing cannot be overstated. Quite apart from the moral question of whether similar crimes should ever be punished with dissimilar sanctions, there are purely practical considerations such as the potentially devastating impact on the morale of prisoners in jails and penitentiaries. The discontent arising from the realization by prisoner A that he is serving triple the time handed out to prisoner B for a similar offense is the stuff that prison riots are made of.

Chapter 4 looks at the question of disparity in general terms. For example: What is the difference between discretion and disparity? How have various authorities viewed the disparity problem? Some of the major independent variables introduced in sentencing studies are reviewed on the basis of a tripartite division into variables that are related to the court, to the defendant, and to the cultural environment, all within a spatial framework. It is emphasized that the spatial importance of variables changes from one context to the next, and it can never be assumed that any individual parameter will necessarily provide a significant degree of geographical explanation.

The role of the prosecutor--the district attorney--in the sentencing process is examined in Chapter 5. It is argued that the prosecutor's work is essentially hidden from public view; while the judge has the nominal responsibility for sentencing, he normally accepts the recommendation of the prosecutor and thus abdicates the task of sentencing. A comparison of violent crimes in two metropolitan counties in Oklahoma is used to suggest that the relative toughness of the prosecutor may result in substantial sentencing differences between jurisdictions.

Further sentencing examples are developed in Chapter 6. A geographical overview of sentencing in the federal court districts is presented in the first part of the chapter, along with models of sentencing patterns, based on legally relevant and irrelevant variables. Then drug felonies in Oklahoma are analyzed on the basis of a prima facie regionalization of the state. It is argued that eastern and western Oklahoma have different cultural traditions, and that sentencing should reflect this difference since judges and prosecutors are elected officials and theoretically mirror the values and expectations of their constituents. A sharp difference in sentencing between regions is indeed apparent, but the expected pattern is reversed, probably as a result of the overwhelming influence of metropolitan areas, and the importance of individual prosecutors in those counties. Another possibility, not investigated in Chapter 6, is that so many drug offenders are sons and daughters of the white middle class that sentencing patterns based on regional attitudes toward drug use are confounded--the drug problem is perceived as being so close to home that leniency occurs where normally it would not. This may be particularly likely in rural counties where social networks are extensive and long established, and include members of the criminal justice establishment. In the major metropolitan districts, on the other hand, offenders are part of a crowd and have no claim on the sentiments of police, prosecutors, or judges. Some additional examples of spatial sentencing patterns are presented, including those in the states of Iowa, New York, and California.

In the final chapter, suggestions are presented for the reform and reorganization of the courts. Courts are examined in terms of their administrative functions--that is, how they are set up and how effective they are in providing their services. The focus is on the federal system, to illustrate how the circuit and district courts are organized and function. By using a number of statistical measures of caseload performance and judgeship/population ratios, the geographic variations are illustrated. These variations are used to suggest and support reforms in the judicial machinery, those that call for both realignment and the allocation of new judgeships. The recent congressional proposals covered in the discussion are aimed at smoothing out the rough wrinkles in the judicial machinery that now exists.

The authors recognize that it is not enough to caterwaul and catalog; therefore, whenever possible, constructive suggestions to remedy problems have been advocated. It is also recognized that perfection will not be achieved--there will always be occurrences in the patterns of laws and in the administration of justice that may be regarded as systematic manifestations of inequity or some other abuse. Our points are that such inequities and abuses can be minimized, and that there may be alternative approaches to the legal organization of space and the application of laws. We hope that this modest work will at least provide a provocation for other geographers and other social scientists to look critically at the criminal justice system in their region and to raise questions about spatial inequities.

NOTES

1. John Fraser Hart, "The Middle West," Annals, Association of American Geographers 62 (1972): 280-81.

2. National Advisory Commission on Criminal Justice Standards and Goals, Courts (Washington, D.C.: U.S. Government Printing Office, 1973), p. 68.

3. "Rape and Death," Newsweek, July 11, 1977, p. 48.

2

A cursory examination of laws within the United States reveals one basic finding, their geographic variation.[1] Of the hundreds of civil and criminal statutes existing throughout the nation, there are many that are similar in wording but different in interpretation. There are equally as many that vary from one location (county or state) to another. That variation in codifying and interpreting laws is related to the prevailing social climate, which is evident in the forms of behavior that are acceptable and in the judgment rendered when cases are before judges and juries. It is this variation that accounts for an incident being considered a petty offense in one county or city and a serious one in a contiguous political unit or another part of the United States. A form of behavior, whether involving abortions, gambling, or pollution of streams, may be legal or approved in one setting but condemned or disapproved of in another.

In order to better understand the geographic dimensions of statutes, three major themes are treated in this chapter. First, we shall examine the concept of regional social philosophy and how this philosophy varies across the nation. This provides a background for the social climate of places and gives meaning to the statutes and administration of justice that have evolved. The second concept discussed is that of spatial rights--that is, how the statutes are defined on a locational basis and how they affect the actions and behaviors of groups and individuals. Third, we shall treat the geographic variation in statutes at local and state levels. Examples are taken from contemporary society to illustrate the wrinkles in the geographic surface for various criminal, civil, and social statutes. The overall objective of this chapter is to present the geographic methodology and perspective for examining statutes and the legal system. That perspective is evident in subsequent chapters focusing on jury selection, sentencing, and court administration.

REGIONAL SOCIAL PHILOSOPHY

The geographic dimensions of statutes are best understood in light of the settlement history and social thought in different parts of the United States. Since different sections or regions were settled by a variety of groups at various times, the prevailing social philosophy acquired a regional character.[2] To comprehend the variation today between New England and the Deep South, or between the Middle West and Southwest, the initial timing of the settlement, its location, and the group or groups responsible for early thought need to be examined. Ideas regarding life, property, and government as set down in statutes did not evolve overnight; rather, they were often amended and changed as new settlers entered a region and exerted an influence on the social order. Not infrequently there were mixtures of settlers in the East, South, or Middle West--for example, those from central and northern Europe who settled in the rural Middle West. Groups also migrated from areas within the United States. In California the northern two-thirds was settled by former New Englanders and middle westerners while the southern part became a destination for those from the South. Multiple migration streams, whether from Europe or areas within the United States, had an impress on social philosophy and, in particular, judicial philosophy in different portions of the nation. Each stream not only represented a given number of people moving from a given origin to a known or unknown destination, but a transfer of ideas and a social philosophy as well. The cultural baggage that New Englanders took to the upper Great Lakes states, or that Germans took to Pennsylvania and the Middle West, or that small farmers from the Deep South carried to southern California contained views regarding religious freedom, individual rights, acceptable forms of punishment, and the role local and the federal government play in society. Thus these new philosophies were juxtaposed with existing philosophies in the new location and became integral parts of the prevailing regional philosophy that evolved.

The formation of regional social philosophies may be considered as layers of cake. Each subsequent layer represents a new culture that has had an impact on the existing thought. Since for the past three centuries, not all areas of the nation have been settled by people from the same parts of Europe or Africa, nor from the same parts of the United States, the layers of the cake are expected to vary in thickness and complexity. That layering continues into the present. The two most recent examples are the migration from rural to urban areas in all parts of the nation and the massive movement by northerners to sunbelt states. That influx of northeasterners and middle westerners into the South and Southwest has had a

significant impact on the changes in regional philosophy in such
places as southern California and the Deep South and border states.
The new migrants into the South have been influential not only in
contesting many of the traditionally accepted notions regarding
minorities and civil rights, but in voting for proposals and political
candidates that were in sharp contrast to the region's prevailing
philosophy.

The best discussion on existing regional philosophies is done
by a political scientist, Daniel Elazar.[3] He examines the "political
geology" of the United States in terms of three major political cultures: individualistic, moralistic, and traditionalistic. Their extent is nationwide as throughout history the impact of one of these
three or of a combination of two can be seen as having been identified with specific locations (cities or states). Not unexpectedly,
there has been a significant layering or blending in some sections,
much more so in some places than others. Thus, mapping the location of these regional political cultures either within states or among
the states reflects the overlapping that exists (see Map 2.1).

Elazar's classification identifies the regional political culture.
It is meant to serve basically as a descriptive tool to aid in examining why different regions, states, and cities have a particular
philosophy. While the three broad cultures and their various combinations are useful in studying the views held on politics and politicians, they are also useful to help identify regional variations in
attitudes toward individuals, overall society, and the role of government. These are integral elements in Elazar's discussion and, as
such, aid in providing a basis from which to identify the geography
of statutes at different levels in the United States.

The individualistic political culture stresses the importance
of the individual in society whether in terms of private initiative or
government programs. The individual officeholder's function is to
support programs that insure and guarantee the importance of private citizens. This culture is found mainly in the central Middle
West and the Mid-Atlantic states, with less concentration in the
Great Plains and the West. It is frequently associated with the traditionalistic culture in Texas and Oklahoma and with the moralistic
philosophy in parts of the Northeast and New England.

The moralistic culture is dominant in New England, the northern Middle West, northern Great Plains, and portions of the Pacific
Northwest and central Rocky Mountains. The underlying character-
istic of this political culture is the emphasis on society rather than
the individual. Politics is important to the development of a pros-
perous society, and the duty of elected officials is to support programs that promote a good life for all citizens. Government has a
moral obligation to see that its programs and conduct support all

MAP 2.1: Regional Distribution of Political Cultures

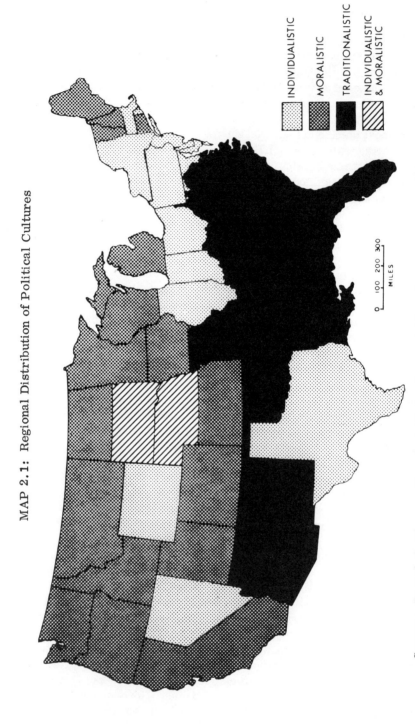

INDIVIDUALISTIC

MORALISTIC

TRADITIONALISTIC

INDIVIDUALISTIC
& MORALISTIC

0 100 200 300
MILES

Source: Daniel J. Elazar, American Federalism: A View from the States, 2d ed. (New York: Thomas Crowell, 1972), pp. 106–07.

citizens. Politicians are thus less committed to vote on party lines; nonpartisanship is common.

The traditionalistic political culture, as the term implies, identifies a precommercial and preindustrial social order. It has a strong regional flavor, being tied to the South (Deep South and rim states). It also exists in the southern parts of Ohio, Indiana, and Illinois, as well as in Arizona and southern California. The culture views family ties and social ties as being especially important, and considers government the domain of a small elite, often with family ties. Political parties are not overly important, and citizen involvement is not encouraged; those elected provide a custodial role rather than introducing and supporting new social programs. A traditional or conservative philosophy prevails in the views elected officials have not only of government, but of citizens. There is strong distaste for outside interference in social and political matters and for bureaucracies, as both run counter to the elite social order that makes decisions.

The nation today may be thought of as having felt the impress of these three cultures and their various combinations in different rural areas, cities, states, and sections. Rural-urban and interregional migration that went north-south or east-west, coupled with advances in communication and technology, have been instrumental in explaining the regional social philosophies that exist (see Map 2.2). It is significant that interpretation of the contemporary social landscape is still strongly affected by the cultural antecedents of groups that settled in certain rural areas or cities one or two centuries ago. Three broad migration streams can be identified; each had an imprint on the social philosophies that developed, and is still useful in explaining present variations in laws and social behaviors. Each major stream has numerous tributaries and distributaries of varying magnitude and direction.

The first broad cultural pattern represents settlement in New England, the Great Lakes, and, subsequently, the Pacific Northwest. Puritan and Yankee settlers were responsible for early social thought that centered in New England. The early settlers' religion was an important part of their life; it was involved in a number of moral issues such as education, abolition of slavery, and political participation. New England settlers who later moved to the northern Middle West mixed mainly with northern Europeans, especially Scandinavians. Both groups shared similar views of society and government--namely, promoting progressive political and societal schemes and legislation. With the movement of these settlers westward late in the last century, their progressive views became associated with parts of the northern Great Plains, northern Rocky Mountains, Pacific Northwest, and northern California.

MAP 2.2: General Migration of Cultural Streams across the United States

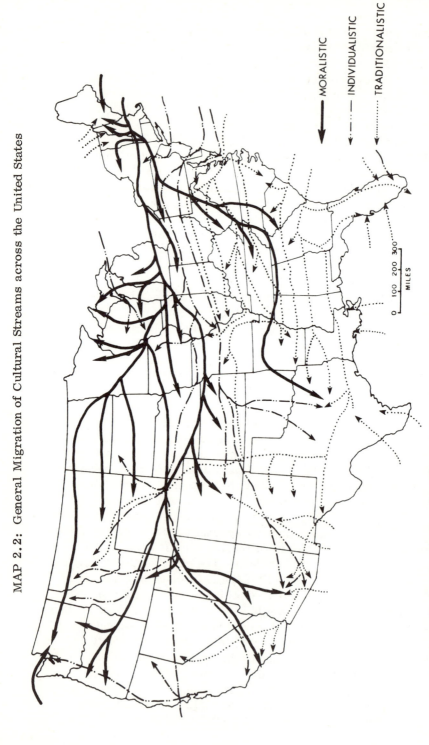

MORALISTIC
INDIVIDUALISTIC
TRADITIONALISTIC

0 100 200 300
MILES

Source: Daniel J. Elazar, American Federalism: A View from the States, 2d ed. (New York: Thomas Crowell, 1972), pp. 110–11.

The second major stream began with the original settlers in the Middle Atlantic states who came mainly from England, Germany, and other parts of central Europe. Some mixed with northern Europeans to form pluralistic political cultures in Pennsylvania and Ohio. To these settlers individualism in politics, society, and personal philosophy was very important, a trait that was reflected in the movement of these Middle Atlantic settlers and their descendants into the central Midwest, the central Great Plains, and lands farther west.

The third major stream was associated with the southern states where the economy was devoted primarily to agriculture rather than industry or commerce. The system of agriculture developed was plantation centered, and incorporated slavery, an ingredient strictly against the grain of residents and states to the north. This landed-gentry system stressed social elites and class separation, rather than the individual in society. Also, it subjected large numbers of indigent immigrant laborers to a less-than-human status in society. This philosophy was concentrated not only in the southern region from Virginia and Kentucky to eastern Texas, Louisiana, and northern Florida, but in the southern parts of Ohio, Indiana, and Illinois as well.

These streams and their tributaries (shown in Map 2.2) mainly identify the transfer of people, ideas, and philosophies in the last century. During this century additional streams have appeared that account for changes in a region's social philosophy. Two that have been briefly described previously are the rural-urban migration and migration to sunbelt states. Movement into large and small urban centers has occurred since the early part of the century in New England, the Middle West, the Northeast and the Mid-Atlantic states, the Pacific Northwest, and California. Urban populations swelled as a result not only of internal migration, which in some cases was substantial as millions of rural blacks moved to the industrial north, but also of immigration. Eastern, central, and southern European immigrants who came to cities in New York, Pennsylvania, Massachusetts, Ohio, Michigan, and Illinois also had an influence on the regional attitudes that emerged. More recently the migration of the elderly to sunbelt cities, especially in Florida, Arizona, and California, has had an impact on the social climate of cities where they constitute a significant segment of the population. This also applies to the mass migration of college and university students to communities where they represent a substantial number; they have affected the passage of certain statutes, the levels of punishment, and the administration of justice. Other recent migrations have added layers to the cake in specific cities and regions; some layers have blended readily into the existing mix, while others have failed because the cultural philosophies were immiscible and unpalatable.

SPATIAL RIGHTS

Each society had as part of its structure views on what were considered rights of individuals, acceptable and unacceptable forms of behavior and punishment, and the role governments played in the daily lives of citizens and in the transactions of business and politics. Statutes represent a framework within which individuals and groups operated according to agreed upon standards. The significance of this perspective from a social geography orientation was that the interpretation of rights and behavior exhibited a distinct geographic character. It was not only the statutes placed on the books that varied, but also their interpretation from one spatial unit to another. Thus we discover that while many political units, such as states, have statutes regarding marriage and divorce, or capital punishment, or the maximum sentences for particular crimes, the geographic pattern of these laws reveals striking variation. This spatial variation may mean a sharp separation in the enactment of certain statutes, their interpretation, and levels of punishment between contiguous counties, cities, and states. For example, the federal Constitution has not been previously, and still is not, interpreted the same way in the North as in the South, whether in matters affecting equal education for blacks or equal employment opportunities, welfare and medical programs, or housing. The enforcement of Supreme Court decisions regarding criminal rights and those of women and minorities is subject to the interpretation of local and state elected and/or appointed officials. Their perspective, in large part fashioned through the prevailing social philosophy of the jurisdiction (county or state) they serve, may be at odds with judgments rendered by federal legislation or Supreme Court decisions.

Since statutes are defined on the basis of some spatial unit, be it county or state or nation, each individual can be considered to have spatial rights. That is, the rights the individual enjoys, if permitted to participate in an open society and to migrate freely between varying locations, will be defined by where he or she is at a particular point in time. Wherever one works, lives, and travels there is a series of laws that are place specific; they define the societal and judicial system for residents in those spaces. The individual who chooses to be mobile would thus be affected by statutes in each new location. This applies to most citizens who are both socially and spatially mobile. The guarantees of spatial mobility as provided in the federal and state constitutions have not always applied to all citizens. Blacks, Mexican-Americans, Indians, and women have frequently found that their rights depended on where they were at a given time. They were denied equality with other members of society, whites in the case of minorities, or men in

the case of women, because of social and legal barriers erected to
restrict their equal and full participation in voting, education, employment, housing, public accommodation, estate settlement, and
the administration of justice. Those rights and privileges that were
legally guaranteed or abridged depended on the prevailing social
climate and the wishes of those in decision-making positions in society (members of state legislatures and city councils, county and
state judges).

The spatial character of rights historically is best documented
by the statutes that affected minorities, especially blacks and women.
Prior to a series of Supreme Court decisions, blacks throughout the
nation found that they enjoyed one set of rights in one state and another set elsewhere (see Map 2.3). For example, Minnesota provided guarantees of quality education, improved housing, public
accommodation, registration and voting, and equal employment long
before Mississippi and New York provided such guarantees before
Alabama did. Improved economic and social conditions in northern
liberal or progressive states were instrumental in attracting southern rural blacks to northern industrial states. Discrepancies at the
state level continued even after a series of Supreme Court decisions
attempted to erase the regional and state differences. In a similar
vein the rights of women have represented diversity among the states
throughout history. Wyoming and Utah had women's suffrage decades
earlier than did Illinois, Ohio, and New York. Nine states in the
South, from Maryland to Louisiana, never did ratify the Nineteenth
Amendment to the Constitution. As of mid-1977 the proposed equal
rights amendment, which is designed to provide greater equality in
such matters as hiring, promotion, estate settlement, and child
care, has been passed by legislatures in 35 states. Women who live
in a state that has not approved this proposed amendment, and they
are mainly in southern states, therefore do not enjoy the same rights
and privileges of those who live elsewhere. [4] All women will not
have the same rights until at least 38 states approve the proposed
amendment; until then women in Utah, Illinois, Florida, and Alabama,
for example, will not enjoy the same rights as those in California,
Michigan, New York, Montana, and 31 other states. Additional examples can be cited where the spatial rights vary from one location
to another. A selected number of varying statutes are treated in the
following section. What is noteworthy in examining rights is the influence of jurisdictional limits. That is, the boundaries, be they
county or state, can be separate political units that have different
statutes, but also differing interpretations for the same statute. The
geography of statutes is important today for many individuals and
groups who are subject to the historical and contemporary interpretation of social conditions and behaviors. Even today the rights

MAP 2.3: Location of De Jure School Segregation Prior to 1954 Supreme Court Decision Outlawing Segregation

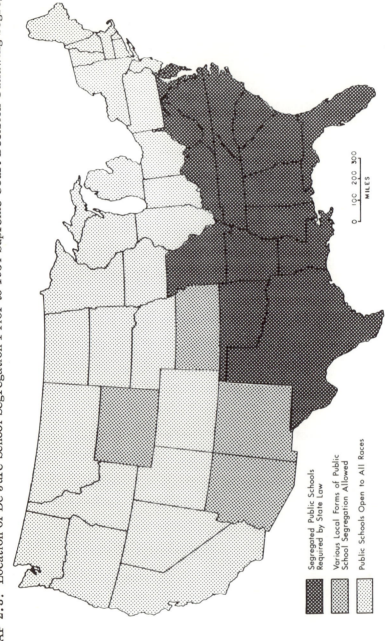

Segregated Public Schools
Required by State Law

Various Local Forms of Public
School Segregation Allowed

Public Schools Open to All Races

0 100 200 300
MILES

Source: J. Dennis Lord, Spatial Perspectives on School Desegregation and Busing (Washington, D.C.: Association of American Geographers, Resource Papers for College Geography [No. 77-3], 1977), pp. 3; reprinted by permission.

MAP 2.4: States Having Ratified Equal Rights Amendment, 1977

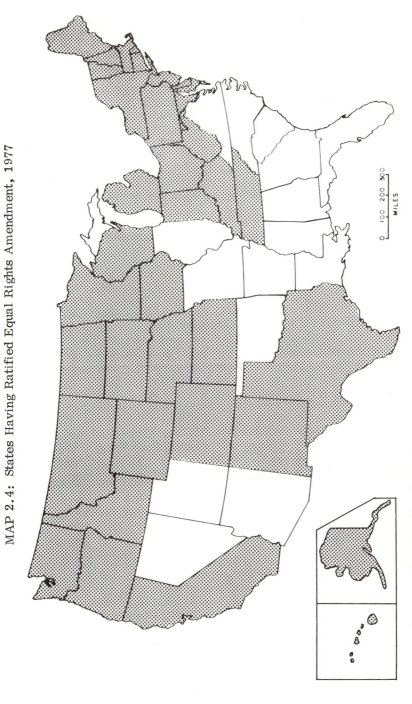

Source: Compiled by the authors.

for the elderly, women, minorities, the handicapped, criminals, businesses, and environmental polluters will vary from one spatial unit to another. In early 1976 the U.S. Bureau of Prisons identified Arkansas, Maryland, Mississippi, and Massachusetts as violating the constitutional rights of prisoners.[5] State programs for the elderly do not provide the same services (dental and optometric care) in Oklahoma, Arkansas, and Wyoming (poor coverage) as they do in Pennsylvania and North Carolina (good coverage).[6] Cancer victims who wish to use laetrile in their treatment cannot obtain it in 36 states, as of mid-1977; those in such states as Indiana, Louisiana, and Delaware can use it legally. Those individuals and groups who are mobile discover that there are no uniform guarantees; rather, rights vary with different locations. Many of the regional, state, and local discrepancies or wrinkles have been erased or eroded through Supreme Court decisions; this provision of equal protection regardless of location, prevailing regional philosophy, or social history is the reason for judgments being handed down by the highest court. The Supreme Court recognized the mobility of Americans and their national awareness of political and social developments, and for this reason gave a nationwide interpretation to such thorny issues as residency requirements for voting and welfare, reapportionment, reciting of prayers in school, open housing, equal employment, and education. In these decisions the court eliminated the state-by-state variations that in some cases were considerable.

In short, we discover that the political organization of space, or how space is divided and subdivided for administrative purposes, is directly related to the rights of the individuals occupying it and to the statutes by which their behavior and actions are governed.[7] Citizens are affected by the county, city, and state where they are residents and by guarantees provided under the Constitution. The situation may become complicated not only for highly mobile Americans who frequently move between regions of varying social philosophies, but also for groups that are under a complex jurisdictional arrangement. This is the case for many American Indians who are under the aegis of a variety of tribal, state, and federal authorities. Where they reside will affect what jurisdiction they are under. Utah and South Dakota Indians are under the jurisdiction of all three levels of authority; Wyoming and North Dakota Indians are only affected by tribal and federal administrations. In 1972 there were 45 states with state jurisdiction over their Indian populations, 16 with federal, and 14 with tribal jurisdiction (see Map 2.5).[8]

MAP 2.5: Indian Rights

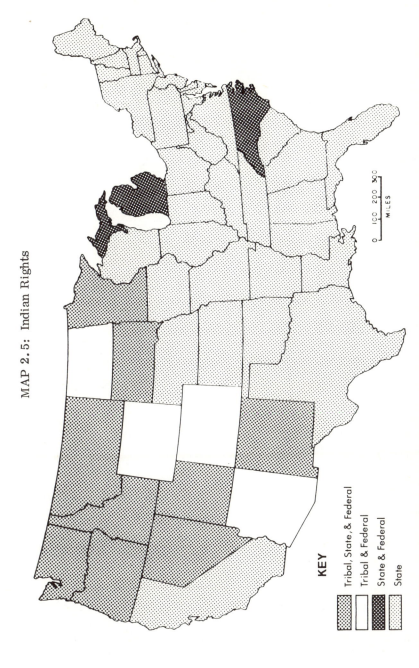

KEY

Tribal, State, & Federal

Tribal & Federal

State & Federal

State

Source: Theodore W. Taylor, The States and Their Indian Cultures (Washington, D.C.: Department of the Interior, Bureau of Indian Affairs, 1972), p. 177.

0 100 200 300
MILES

GEOGRAPHIC VARIATIONS

In this section the focus is on the variation that exists in statutes at different levels. Examples are selected from among local
and state statutes. The objective is threefold: to illustrate the
variation that exists, to identify the influence of original settlement
streams on the prevailing social climate, and to underscore how the
geographic variation affects the behavior and actions of residents,
whether they be members of city councils, legislatures, juries, or
the judicial profession.

Local Level

Counties and communities across the country have established
their own statutes either by unwritten laws that later became codified
in formal language, by the wishes of ruling elites or majorities, by
referendums, or by constantly changed court decisions. Local
variations, as expected, are the result even in contiguous counties.
Several examples illustrate this diversity. The sale of alcoholic
beverages in the South is marked by laws that have an almost random
appearance.[9] Driving from north to south in Georgia, one passes
through counties that are completely dry, some that are completely
wet, or some where only beer and wine are sold. In Arkansas a
tourist traveling east-west passes through counties and cities that
are either completely wet or dry (see Map 2.6). Local political
decisions govern what is sold in this fundamentalist and politically
conservative state. The pattern at the county level is complicated
by precincts or townships where some beverages are sold while
others are prohibited.

Local options are established to govern the sale of certain
books and movies. Obscene or girlie magazines have been available
in bookstores where local ordinances permit their sale. In more
than one metropolitan area across the nation, whether Playboy,
Playgirl, Hustler, Oui, or other magazines of a more pornographic
nature are sold depends on community standards and local objection
to their sale. Not infrequently, adjacent suburbs and townships have
conflicting ordinances. If an individual is unable to purchase a
specific magazine in one locale, a short trip to an adjacent one will
usually permit the purchase. Some movies also have been prohibited
in certain cities and parts of cities because their racial, sexual,
violent, or pronographic nature conflicts with local religious and
philosophical standards. The term "banned in Boston" was meant to
illustrate the variations in attitudes toward certain kinds of movies,
books, and adult entertainment. Movie producers and distributors

MAP 2.6: Wet and Dry Counties in Arkansas

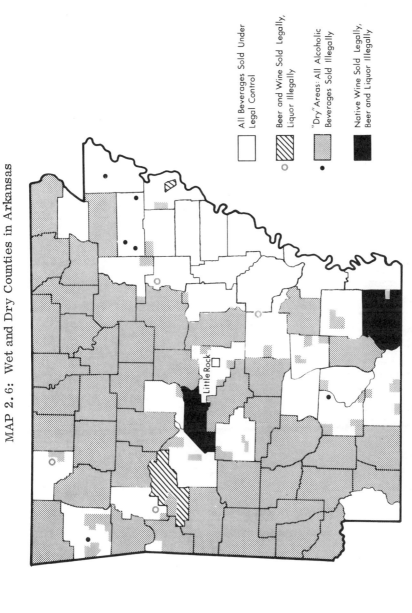

All Beverages Sold Under
Legal Control

Beer and Wine Sold Legally,
Liquor Illegally

"Dry" Areas: All Alcoholic
Beverages Sold Illegally

Native Wine Sold Legally,
Beer and Liquor Illegally

Source: Stanley D. Brunn, Geography and Politics in America (New York: Harper and Row, 1974),
p. 203, from data provided by State of Arkansas, Department of Alcoholic Beverage Control, 1973.

recognize that certain kinds of movies will not be widely accepted
or long running in all locations. Sexually explicit and morally
degrading films are likely to have a restricted distribution, possibly
primarily to college and university communities, while family and
outdoor adventure films will be more popular across the social
spectrum of the nation and in metropolitan areas. A number of film
distributors and owners of bookstores have discovered the meaning
of community standards after being arrested for showing specific
movies and peddling certain books.

The religious heritage of a community is an underlying cause
of many variations in statutes. Blue laws in cities in New England
and the Northeast not only prohibited the sale of liquor and other
retail items, but also affected the termination of weekend baseball
games. Laws are still on the books in the New York City area that
forbid the washing of cars on Sunday on Long Island. There are
Sabbath provisions as well that permit Jewish shopowners to operate
on Sunday provided they close another day. Areas of the rural
Middle West and South where fundamentalism is strong were able to
prevent the opening of stores on Sunday. However, this policy
changed with the adoption of a greater secular emphasis by these
religious groups and with the realization that large shopping centers
in nearby regional centers were not affected by such ordinances.

The major example where local statutes affected social behavior was in the policies that were designed to exclude certain groups
--blacks, Jews, and Mexican-Americans. Where such ordinances
were enacted and enforced, they affected the sales of property and
the use of public facilities. In short, these restrictive clauses or
covenants denied opportunities for certain groups to enjoy full participation in the social spaces of a community. While many of these
clauses and covenants have been declared unconstitutional since the
1960s, a number remain de facto as attempts to maintain community
standards according to the wishes of an elite or majority. Two recent developments that underscore the persistence of attempts to
eliminate unfair local ordinances are the existence of redlining,
whereby local banks and investment houses deny loans to individuals
planning to develop certain areas, and the denial of equal housing
and employment for homosexuals. Redlining is an ordinance that is
not codified, but is de facto and, to many blacks, carries the same
meaning as previous unwritten laws imposed by the whites in some
communities that attempted to keep them on their own side of the
tracks. Ordinances banning homosexuals from communities or re-
stricting their residential spaces are seen as similar to the zoning
restrictions formerly placed on Jews, blacks, Mexican-Americans,
and other minority groups.

A significant feature of the geography of statutes is the importance of boundaries. Boundaries are decided by individuals and groups and are not natural. County lines, township borders, suburban city limits, and state boundaries have been established for ease in administering functions in a society. They are important in understanding statutes in that they apply to residents living within their spaces. Laws inherently have a geographic dimension. At the local level the boundaries may serve to separate widely varying statutes, interpretations of the same statutes, and degrees of punishment for violation. In this case the boundaries are important in that they affect interaction and behavior. The opportunities or rights are different on each side of the boundary. Residents who are of a similar social background, and who cross the boundary daily to work, shop, enjoy recreation, or visit would find that political boundary significant. It may even constitute a barrier that precludes taking advantage of opportunities given others in the society, such as the ability to purchase quality housing or to enroll a child in a particular school system. Other citizens may perceive that there are opportunities in places across a boundary that make those places attractive, such as the presence of illicit activities or of cheaper or illegal goods that are unavailable in the place of one's residence. In the South boundary residents have traveled across the county boundary to obtain legal alcoholic beverages; in the Middle West and West, to find brothels. Those numerous boundaries that are permeable--that is, crossed without any social or political significance --are not at issue here. It is those at the local or state level where the border distinction is important. In Prohibition days a hasty retreat across the border was critical to those making moonshine and other then-illegal beverages. The high concentration of distilleries and distributors in borderline locations was not without reason. Many an individual criminal or organization engaged in subtle or overt criminal activities recognizes the importance of understanding the geography of laws. It affects not only when and where crimes occur, but where the arrest is made and the trial held. This applies to those operating at local levels or on an interstate scale.

State Level

There are dozens of statutes in states that affect the lives of residents living within their borders. The Constitution provides that certain duties with regard to society will be the responsibility of the individual states. With this provision, it comes as no surprise that there is often little agreement on statutes or their enforcement

among the 50 states. In the historical evolution of the nation, states
have been regarded as key elements in the nation's political organization and social development. Lack of communication between
states and a strong desire to make each state's constitution and
rights speak for its own residents led to a greater amount of diversity than uniformity or agreement. The political cultures (outlined
previously) that were established and evolved in each state that was
carved out accounted for social conditions and the population in a
state being perceived slightly differently than elsewhere. States
that may have had a progressive social philosophy were likely to
pass legislation and enforce statutes on individual rights, while such
rights may never have been heard of in states with a traditional
agrarian philosophy. There were almost as many possible interpretations of some issues as there were states. Therefore, a cartographic pattern showing the availability of a particular service
such as abortion or equal housing for blacks once resembled a patch-
work quilt. More complex patterns resulted in cases of punishment
for selected crimes such as marijuana possession, first-degree
murder, or sexual offenses such as general lewdness. Political
cultures, similar settlement histories, economic orientation, and
political philosophy proved insufficient to provide a simple rational
explanation for the patterns that have emerged.

States are charged with protecting citizens and their space in
numerous areas. They determine residency requirements for office
seekers, what offices shall be elected ones, eligibility requirements
for certain medical programs for the elderly, rights for young
adults, educational requirements, and licensing standards for pro-
fessionals such as beauticians, lawyers, morticians, and veterinar-
ians. Interstate variations are common even among adjacent states
settled at the same time by identical migration streams. One major
arena where state discrepancies are widespread, even to the point of
being almost ludicrous, are those statutes that govern marriage and
divorce. A close reading of the marriage requirements from state
to state reveals three features: in some cases the minimum age
varies considerably, the waiting period for obtaining a license varies,
and there are often different requirements for males and females
(see Map 2.7). Young women who are at least 14 years old may
marry in Alabama, New York, and Utah with parental consent, but
not in other states; they must be at least 18 in Indiana and Washington. Men must be at least 14 to marry with parental consent in New
Hampshire, and 15 in Missouri, but have to be 18 in 17 other states.
There is no waiting period for obtaining a license in 22 states, but a
five-day wait in Maine, Oklahoma, and Wisconsin, and a seven-day
wait in Oregon. The types of tests required also vary. Four states
require none. Divorce requirements also vary (see Map 2.7). The

MAP 2.7: Marriage Laws by State

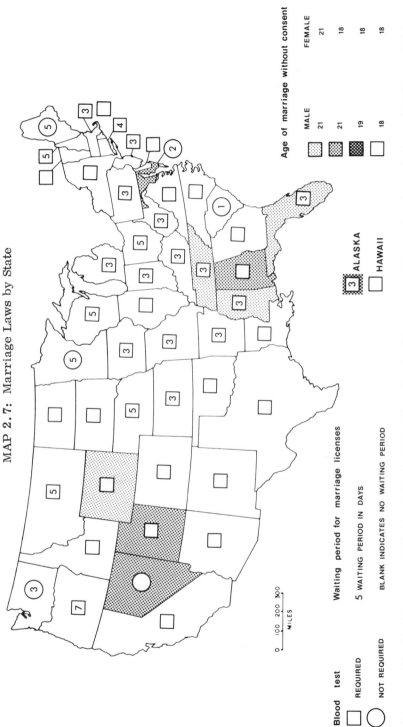

Source: World Almanac and Book of Facts 1977 (New York: Newspaper Enterprise Association, 1977), p. 961.

grounds for divorce, the waiting period, and the required time before remarriage exhibit substantial spatial variations. Recent reforms and attempts to standardize marriage and divorce statutes have still left wide discrepancies among the states.

Religious, social, and political variations account for many of the social codes passed by state legislatures. This is especially the case in laws governing moral actions and criminal behavior; the way in which a state and its residents value human life, the individual's position in society, the role of men and women, varying lifestyles that are a departure from the majority, corporal punishment, and rehabilitation all are reflected in the interpretation of a crime and suitable punishment. It is expected that with the numerous migration streams crossing the nation and influencing different regions, state statutes on criminal behavior and activity will vary.

The variation in state statutes for criminal offenses can be demonstrated by examining the severity of penalties imposed (see Map 2.8). Prior to the Supreme Court's 1972 ruling abolishing capital punishment for murder or rape, when imposed by a jury, the maximum penalty for first-degree murder varied considerably from state to state. A number of states in the Northeast and Middle West with a moralistic political culture had already abolished capital punishment. In many more in the South and Middle West, where traditionalistic and individualistic cultures developed, the maximum penalty was electrocution or lethal gas. A recent trend to reinstitute capital punishment in at least a dozen states in the South and West has been supported mainly by states with strong conservative and traditional regional philosophies. This is also the case for certain violent crimes such as rape. The pattern of states that had capital punishment as the maximum penalty for rape corresponds almost perfectly with the states with a traditionalistic political culture. This strong penalty reflected a regional social philosophy (in the South) that was fundamentalist in religion and agrarian in social values, fostered racial separation, and held to a strict interpretation of laws. In the case of rape the charges and punishments were often administered in large part against the rural poor and blacks.

The pattern showing the punishment for marijuana on a state level is much more complicated than the five classes of criminal acts used. The maximum jail sentence that a resident of a state could receive in the early 1970s (prior to much reform and the decriminalization of the drug) exhibited much more diversity among states than uniformity. Sentences for possession could run for less than 90 days in Michigan, for not more than six months in Iowa and Utah, for not more than ten years in Indiana, and not more than 15 in Rhode Island. At this time, Texas had a maximum penalty of life imprisonment for those convicted of possession. Penalties also

MAP 2.8: Criminal Offenses and Severity of Penalties: Prisoners under Sentence of Death, by Jurisdiction, 1974

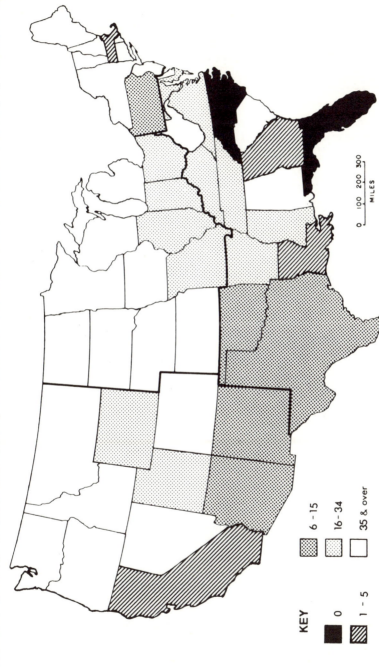

KEY

6 - 15

0

16 - 34

1 - 5

35 & over

MILES

0 100 200 300

Source: U.S. Department of Justice, Law Enforcement Assistance Administration, National Criminal Justice Information and Statistics Service, Sourcebook on Criminal Justice Statistics, 1976 (Washington, D.C.: U.S. Government Printing Office, 1977), p. 763.

varied with second and third offenses, in cases of selling to minors,
and in convictions for pushing. Recent revision of criminal codes
has shortened the maximum and minimum jail sentences and fines
that could be imposed. Alaska, South Dakota, and Oregon are
among the states that have reduced fines and/or prison sentences.[10]
Local community standards still are important in the sentence meted
out. University of Michigan students in Ann Arbor once could get by
with paying a $5 fine if convicted.

Numerous other examples of criminal statutes that vary at
state levels could be discussed and illustrated cartographically.
Consensual sex offenses defined as adultery, cohabitation, fornica-
tion, and crimes against nature have different fines and jail sentences on a state-to-state basis.[11] What is tolerated in one state
may be a serious offense in another. Penalties for robbery, burglary, larceny, auto theft, and manslaughter are defined in a state's
criminal code. The fines or prison sentences may have been codified in the last century according to the then-prevailing social
philosophy of the state or region. Newer and more recent ideas
brought from outside the state or region may or may not have had
an impact on bringing changes in statutes. The result of viewing
statutes at the national level is frequently one of diversity and complexity.

SUMMARY

In this chapter the focus has been on providing a basis for
understanding the geography of statutes.[12] That basis has been
laid by examining briefly the cultural heritages and regional social
philosophies that have emerged. Since various racial and ethnic
groups migrated to and settled in different regions, a regional
philosophy developed regarding individual rights, the mores of society, and the role of local and federal governments. Three broad
political and social cultures and various combinations of them
evolved in the United States: the individualistic, moralistic, and
traditionalistic. They are a useful framework from which to examine the concept of spatial rights--that is, where one resides there
is a distinct set of codified actions and behaviors that affect the
acceptance of behaviors and actions of individuals and groups.
Women, blacks, Indians, and other minorities have had, and still
have, rights defined by location. A number of local and state statutes are used to illustrate the geographic diversity that exists.
Some relate to public rights and laws, and others to criminal offenses. The need for considering statutes in a spatial or geographic
context at the local, state, or national level becomes apparent in the

discussion on jury selection methods in the following chapter.
There the geographic dimensions are also significant in civil or
criminal trials.

NOTES

1. For a general discussion on the geographic perspective
on law including that of statutes, see Stanley D. Brunn, Geography
and Politics in America (New York: Harper and Row, 1974), pp.
199-236. Examples of statutes at different levels are discussed and
illustrated cartographically.
    2. The geographic processes in settlement and the resulting
social/cultural patterns are described and succinctly analyzed in
Wilbur Zelinsky, A Cultural Geography of the United States (Englewood Cliffs, N.J.: Prentice-Hall, 1973).
    3. Daniel J. Elazar, American Federalism: A View From
the States (New York: Thomas Crowell, 1972), pp. 103-26.
    4. The geographic rights of women on a state basis are well
tabulated and documented in Shana Alexander, State-by-State Guide
to Women's Legal Rights (Los Angeles: Wollstonecraft, 1975).
What is needed is a series of companion volumes that would outline
the interstate statutes for other members of society: the elderly,
children and juveniles, the handicapped, prisoners, and the indigent.
    5. John Dillin, "Prison 'Rights Revolution' Stirs," Christian
Science Monitor, January 15, 1976, pp. 1, 6.
    6. Selected additional medicaid services, by state, for which
federal financial participation is available are summarized in Information Please Almanac (New York: Simon and Schuster, 1977),
p. 615.
    7. The geographic perspective on the social and political
organization of space is discussed in Brunn, op. cit., pp. 131-76
and in John A. Jakle, Stanley D. Brunn, and Curtis C. Roseman,
Human Spatial Behavior: A Social Geography (North Scituate,
Mass.: Duxbury Press, 1976), pp. 245-75.
    8. Theodore W. Taylor, The States and Their Indian Citi-
zens (Washington, D.C.: Department of the Interior, Bureau of
Indian Affairs, 1972), p. 177. Indian claims, courts, and rights
are among the topics discussed in Lawrence Rosen, ed., "The
American Indian and the Law," Law and Contemporary Problems
46 (1976): 1-223.
    9. John Fraser Hart, The Southeastern United States (Prince-
ton, N.J.: Van Nostrand, 1967), Figure 6, "Alcoholic Beverages."
    10. Clayton Jones, "'Decriminalization' Efforts Pushed:
Marijuana Use Gaining Wider Leniency in U.S.," Christian Science
Monitor, August 20, 1976, p. 5.

11. The state-by-state variations in penalties for sexual offenses are listed in Richard Rhodes, "Sex and Sin in Sheboygan," Playboy, August 1972, pp. 188-89.

12. From the examples given in different areas of human activity, it is apparent that the geography of statutes covers many other fields such as taxation, estate settlement, corporate law, and environmental rights. Geographers are beginning to pursue research in these areas. The significant contributions of Otis Templer to the study of water rights at local, state, and national levels suggest numerous avenues for future study. See Otis Templer, "Institutional Constraints and Water Resources: Water Rights Adjudication in Texas," Rocky Mountain Social Science Journal 10, no. 3 (1973): 37-45, "Water Law and the Hydrologic Cycle: A Texas Example," Water Resources Bulletin 9 (1973): 273-83, and Institutional Constraints and Conjunctive Management of Water Resources in West Texas, (OWRT) Project No. A-029-TEX, Project Completion Report (Lubbock: Texas Tech University, Water Resources Center, Office of Water Research Technology, 1976).

3

JURY SELECTION

A series of publicized political trials involving Watergate figures, Vietnam War protesters, and political activists have brought issues of justice to the fore in the past few years. At issue are the guarantee of a representative jury, the jury selection methods, and the defense and prosecution strategies used to obtain favorable verdicts. These issues question the constitutional rights of individuals brought to trial as well as the basis of an impartial system of justice. Much of the criticism of the system has focused on criminal trials in which the procedures used to select jurors have included behavioral and demographic profiles of citizens in the community where the trial was held. Some social scientists and attorneys have maintained that these methods manipulate or stack the jury and thereby undermine the credibility of the entire legal system.[1] Others maintain that the input of social and behavioral scientists results in the seating of a higher-quality jury that is more representative.[2]

That justice, methods of selecting jurors, and those seated for a trial reflect spatial and social dimensions is apparent. The location of the trial, requests for changes of venue, the judicial caseload, the pretrial period, the sentencing variations for similar crimes in different districts and states, the behavior patterns of judges, the social and political profiles of communities and districts, and the areas represented by jurors illustrate the importance of space or area in the administration of justice. To understand the inconsistencies, irregularities, and inequalities in the system calls for an examination of the interfaces between geography and justice.

The primary objective of this discussion is to focus on only one common boundary between geography and the law: the methods utilized to select jurors. It is hoped this will suggest possible contributions geographers can offer legal firms, and stimulate additional research. Additional facets could also be examined, such as the

importance of changes of venue or sentencing variations or varying
legal interpretations of criminal and civil codes. Geographers have
only recently begun to investigate the interfaces between social and
political geography and justice.[3] Likewise, other social and behavioral scientists and attorneys are becoming aware of the spatial
facets of justice.[4]

The chapter is divided into five parts. First, the theme of
spatial and social justice is dealt with broadly within the United
States. This introduction is followed by an assessment of methods
used to select citizens for jury duty. Third, some examples of how
social science teams have contributed their skills to the selection of
jurors in several noted trials are discussed. Many inputs are similar to those that geographers might make available to the defense or
prosecution in civil or criminal proceedings. Fourth, some possible
roles are offered for urban social and political geographers who
might pursue research assignments that would aid in selecting jurors
or determining community attitudes. Once these facets have been
considered, it is indeed apparent that there are a number of contributions geographers can offer to improve the overall judicial system as well as aid the defense or prosecution staffs. Models of jury
selection are presented that illustrate the spatial dimensions that
are involved in selecting possible jurors. Finally, the question of
redefining justice is treated.

JUSTICE: SOCIAL AND SPATIAL

The fact that social justice has spatial ramifications has been
acknowledged by many attorneys, scholars, and the general public.
The conviction of blacks by previously all-white juries in the South,
the varying penalties for marijuana possession in Michigan and Texas,
the more lenient laws in Nevada, and the prison sentences meted out
for forgery or auto theft in different court districts reflect a judicial
surface with many wrinkles. The administration and application of
justice are marked not only by regional or interstate or intrastate
contrasts, but by contrasts between social classes as well. The
likelihood of a jury reaching a similar decision in two contrasting
cases--for example, the case of a poor, inner city black who robbed
a branch bank, and that of a wealthy white suburban banker who em-
bezzled his bank's funds--is probably not great. Frequently, those
charged with committing a petty criminal offense that affects few are
given stiffer sentences than white-collar criminals whose actions
affect thousands. These inconsistencies in the administration of
justice are due in part to the residential location of the criminal, his
or her station in life, the site of the crime, and the geographical and
social composition of the jury.

Because of these variations or irregularities, which may be termed injustices, there is a need to examine justice in spatial terms.[5] Where the criminal lives, commits the crime, is tried, and is sentenced reflect the definitions of justice and its administration, possibly at more than one location. The knowledgeable criminal and criminal lawyer are cognizant of the geographical aspects of law and justice. Spatial ramifications become apparent in the community or district where the trial is held, and when race, income, national origin, class, religion, and occupation are reflected in the community attitudes of potential jurors, the temperament of the judges, and the nature of the case itself. Legal teams for the defense and prosecution have recognized these as salient elements in their courtroom questioning and strategies including their recommendations for selecting jurors.[6] Clarence Darrow believed that Prohibitionists, Presbyterians, Baptists, Scandinavians, and the wealthy were more apt to convict "underdog" clients than were Jews, agnostics, Irishmen, and those who liked to laugh.[7] Whereas many lawyers, especially trial lawyers, have relied on their intuition and courtroom skills to identify sympathetic yet impartial jurors, we now find that some legal firms are hiring social scientists to develop community profiles based on census materials and surveys taken in the community. These data measure attitudes toward minority groups, unpopular causes, government policy, and specific issues within the community. Many of these investigations have focused on social and geographic variations within cities and districts.

Some geographers may see the issues raised about social and spatial justice as suggestive of the role individual geographers and the profession as a whole might play in advocacy planning and research. This position may well appeal to the professional geographer, and he or she may prefer to aid defense attorneys in supporting political activists or particular criminal actions; no judgment is passed here on this stance. Rather, the point raised here is intended to provide an understanding of the ways in which rights and the application of justice vary over space. The effects these variations have on individual citizens or group behavior is considered a part of behavioral geography, especially those facets concerned with society and politics. How these variations are seen in the perceptions of justice, measurement of civil rights, class conflict, territoriality, political identification, social cohesion, public consciousness, authority, and government policy are worthwhile avenues for research in social geography and the social sciences in general.

JURY SELECTION PROCEDURES

Two issues arise in connection with the selection of potential jurors. First, what is the base or pool from which the jurors are

drawn?; and second, how representative is the list of persons living
in the community or district where the trials are held? A related
question that is equally important is whether the jury selected after
an examination by the presiding judge and/or attorneys is a cross
section of the community.

According to the federal Jury Selection and Service Act of
1968, persons cannot be excluded from serving on juries because
of race, color, national origin, sex, religion, or economic status.
In essence, a cross section of society is the ideal, but one that is
seldom achieved because of the exclusion of certain groups (blacks
and women previously) or of certain occupations that are excused
from serving. [8] The jury panel is to be selected at random from a
list of persons living in the court district. Usually this procedure
involves the preparation, by the court clerk or jury commissioner,
of a list of potential jurors for an upcoming session. In most cases
the federal courts rely on voter registration lists as the pool. While
it is not necessary that all eligible persons in the community appear
on the list, it should be one that is representative of the area involved.

While using voter registration lists to develop a list of potential jurors at the outset may appear to be the easiest and fairest
method of obtaining a representative sample, there are limitations
to its use. Those citizens who are interested in politics and moti-
vated to participate in referendums or elections would register to
vote. Thus their names would appear on the registration list. However, voting or registration are not franchises that are exercised
uniformly by all groups within a community or district. Rather,
voters have a distinct set of characteristics that separate them from
nonvoters. [9] They are usually better educated, have higher incomes
and higher occupational levels. Young people, minority groups, and
low-income groups, who would tend to vote Democratic, as well as
new residents are least likely to have registered.

These social variations account for irregularities in the registration and voting rates within a community or court district. If
all parts of a community had uniform registration rates, the random
sample of potential jurors would reflect this homogeneous surface.
Since the sample is random it may identify more persons from a
particular ethnic, income, or social group, or political party, because of their proportion of the total population that is registered.
It may be that a socially or geographically stratified sampling frame
would yield a more representative cross section of the community.

A recent study of the potential jurors for federal and state
courts in Rhode Island revealed that their age, sex, and education
levels differed, in some cases measurably, from comparable data
for the overall adult population. [10] Within communities and districts

the rural-urban and inner city-suburban differences also would probably show variations in the percent of adults registered to vote.
When these inequalities exist in the voter lists, they would also bias
the selection of potential jurors who are randomly selected. In short,
while a representative cross section of the community is selected at
random for jury duty, registering to vote, or even voting, is not a
random event.

Women, minority groups, the poor, and the young are the
major groups often not represented according to their proportion of
the population on juries. The Supreme Court has ruled that women
cannot be arbitrarily excluded from jury duty. The sex bias was
documented by the New York City Legal Aid Society in a 1973 suit in
federal court that charged the county clerk and his deputy had vio-
lated civil rights laws in selecting members for the grand jury in
Queens. The list was found discriminatory on the grounds of sex,
race, occupation, and residence. Over 53 percent of the population
in Queens were women, but they comprised only 13 percent of the
grand jury roll in 1972.[11] In late 1976 and early 1977 the New York
State Supreme Court found juries on Staten Island biased; too few
women and blacks were selected for duty. Fifty-one percent of the
potential jurors were women, yet only 15 percent were on jury panels;
29 percent of the population were under 30 years old, yet in November
1976 only two of 103 jurors selected were under 30. As of February
1977 none of the 96 called was under 30 years old.[12] A federal panel
in 1973 ruled invalid a Louisiana law that banned women from jury
duty unless they volunteered. The decision held that the state jury
selection system denied women and men equal protection under the
law. In another case related to age, a Denver juvenile court judge
in 1971 disqualified 360 persons picked as jurors because they were
too old to be representative of the community. Although 24 percent
of the eligible jurors in Denver were between 20 and 30, only 6 percent of those selected were within this bracket.[13] The underrepresentation of blacks on southern and inner city juries, of Mexican-
Americans on jury lists in the Southwest, and of young people in university district juries illustrates similar imbalances in the jury lists
and jurors selected. The U.S. Supreme Court said that unconstitutional discrimination can occur in grand jury selection procedures
in a county, even if a group discriminated against is in the majority.
The case in point involved Hidalgo County, Texas, where Mexican-
Americans (79 percent of the population) were discriminated against
in the grand jury selection system. From 1962 to 1972 they comprised only 39 percent of the grand juries, even though the Spanish-
surname population elected the majority of county officials.[14] Many
members of these groups as well as new residents are excluded from
service because their names do not appear on voter registration lists.

Even with the passage of the Twenty-Sixth Amendment, extending
voting privileges to 18-year-olds, and the passage in 1972 of the
amendment to the Federal Jury Selection and Service Act, which
extended jury service to 18-21-year-olds in federal criminal trials,
there are still 11 states that exclude these young people from jury
duty. They are Alabama, Alaska, Colorado, Louisiana, Mississippi,
Missouri, Nebraska, New Jersey, Rhode Island, South Carolina, and
Vermont.[15]

In some states supplemental sources are used to identify and
select jurors. These may include telephone directories, auto registration lists, and lists of utility customers. New York recently has
added to its juror pool from these additional lists.[16] However, each
of these, likewise, has serious limitations because certain social
groups within a city or state are discriminated against if they do not
have telephones or own automobiles. These gaps would lead to an
underrepresentation of both groups and areas in a random sample.
The New Jersey Assembly in 1972 approved a bill that was designed
to broaden the base for selecting jurors by requiring that jurors be
picked from motor vehicle registration lists (not automobile owner-
ship lists) as well as voter registration lists. Alaska includes lists
of those with hunting and trapping licenses. Colorado uses city
directories and motor vehicle lists as well as voter registration
lists; only felons and those under 18 years of age are excused.

Jury commissioners and county clerks select jurors in some
states. Some of these court-appointed officials have been known to
identify key friends and acquaintances for jury duty, to the exclusion
of large segments of the population. The term "blue ribbon" panels
or juries itself connotes a group of citizens from the higher socioeconomic strata of a community. They may not be representative of
the community in question. In New York City the Manhattan district
attorney in 1974 called for the abolition of the sheriff's jury panel
because it contained 450 of the city's financial elite who avoided
regular jury duty by being appointed to the panel. In other boroughs
jurors were selected at random. Placing members from a particular
social class or region of the community on a list of potential jurors
further violates the representative basis for selecting a cross section of citizens.

The exclusion of certain members of a community from jury
duty may further bias the list of potential jurors and the final jury
selected in criminal or civil cases. Doctors, clergy, politicians,
lawyers, and teachers, who may occupy a sizable segment of the
population in some communities (with respect to class and area) may
be exempt, depending on the state laws. The New Mexico House
passed a bill in 1973 requiring doctors, lawyers, professors, and
ministers to serve on juries. The New Jersey governor vetoed a

measure in 1974 that would have exempted high school, college,
seminary, and vocational students from jury duty. The New York
Assembly in 1971 approved a bill exempting chiropractors from
duty. State statutes exempt fruitgrowers in Virginia, librarians in
Minnesota, lighthouse keepers in Massachusetts, canal operators in
Florida, and funeral directors in New Mexico.[17] Various attempts
are under way to make jury duty mandatory for all eligible citizens.[18]
The innovation of the one day-one trial system is gaining support in
large cities such as Houston and Detroit. It eliminates the lengthy
periods of some trials, an individual's daily appearance in court to
await possible selection, and the distaste for jury duty. This experiment is in response to the numerous complaints regarding selection and jury duty itself.[19]

   The importance of the procedures used to select potential
jurors lies in the degree to which the various social groups and geographic areas are represented on jury lists and on juries themselves
within the community. If the statutes call for individuals to be selected from a representative cross section of the community, and
the jury lists are biased against or weighted in favor of particular
groups or sections of a community, the potential jury will probably
reflect a similar unrepresentative quality. It is possible that low-
income, nonvoting sections of inner cities--populated by recent immigrants or minority group members--rural portions of some districts, and university student housing areas will be underrepresented
on the jury lists. These individuals would then have little chance for
selection. Similar irregularities may appear when age, sex, education, and occupation levels of jurors are compared with regionwide
or neighborhood data published by the census and other public agencies. To the extent that irregularities appear and are permitted to
stand, those brought to trial may not be able to receive a fair trial
from a representative cross section of the community where they
live or where the trial is held.

   There have been a number of cases where the defense has
challenged the composition of the jury because it was unrepresentative of the community in question. Some judges have ruled in favor
of such motions. A Los Angeles Superior Court judge in 1974 held
that the poor were discriminated against in trials within the county
because they were not fairly represented on juries; they were underrepresented on voter registration lists from which jurors were drawn.
The judge ruled in favor of a defense motion that three young blacks
charged with assaulting a police officer could not receive a fair trial
from the impaneled jurors. In a 1973 case the federal district judge
in Montgomery County, Alabama, ruled that discrimination in the
selection of jurors by race, sex, or income level was unconstitutional,
and ordered the county jury commissioner to reconstitute a jury so

that it would represent a cross section of the community.[20] Data
revealed that although 30 percent of the jury-age population in the
county were black, only 12 percent of the potential jurors were.
Women comprised 54 percent of the population, but only 16 percent
of those eligible for jury duty.

In a related case aimed at correcting inequities in the judicial
system, the California State Supreme Court in 1973 ruled that persons charged with criminal offenses have a constitutional right to be
tried by a jury drawn from and composed of a representative cross
section of the residents of the community where the crime was actually committed. This ruling reversed the conviction of an individual who was found guilty of selling marijuana in 1970. In that
year the Los Angeles Superior Court had stipulated that all crimes
committed in the Central Judicial District (31 percent black) should
be tried in the Southwest Judicial District (only 7 percent black) because of the court's overload. Jurors in this particular case were
drawn from the Southwest District only.[21]

SOCIAL SCIENCE INPUTS INTO JURY SELECTION

Psychologists and sociologists have aided defense counsel in a
number of well-known trials including those of Watergate figures,
Angela Davis, Joan Little, the Attica prisoners, Kent State national
guardsmen, and members of the Symbionese Liberation Army (SLA).
In four of the most publicized political trials--involving the Harrisburg Seven, former Attorney General John Mitchell and former Secretary of Commerce Maurice Stans, the Wounded Knee activists,
and Patricia Hearst and William and Emily Harris of the SLA--
social scientists contributed to the defense by preparing community
profiles from pretrial interviews with possible jurors in order to
determine the demographic characteristics of those sympathetic to
the defense. In these and other cases much of the social and behavioral data used were derived from census sources and from telephone and field interviews. The correlations, analyses, and profiles
were used in the voir dire examination in which the judge and/or
prosecuting and defense attorneys question prospective jurors on a
variety of topics. How the examination is conducted, and who con-
ducts it, varies from state to state.[22] The aim of this examination
is to identify those who are impartial but possibly sympathetic to the
defense. Citizens are queried about their attitudes toward the causes
espoused by the defendants, ideas about authority and government,
and views toward minority groups. These responses, along with
racial, ethnic, religious, occupational, and family background data,
are used to match the prospective juror with the pretrial community

behavioral profiles. Some potential jurors are dismissed for bias
and others removed by preemptory challenges where no cause need
be stated. The importance of the voir dire examination is recognized by both parties in a case and the judges themselves.[23] Behavioral and attitudinal data are indeed important indicators in influencing jurors and their verdicts.[24]

The Harrisburg Seven trial in 1972 received national attention
because those individuals involved were charged with plotting to kidnap Henry Kissinger and bomb Pentagon installations. In selecting
Harrisburg the federal government believed it had a good chance of
having these charges sustained, because of the conservative leanings
of the judge, and because of the city's low Catholic population, its
large number of fundamentalist religious sects, Republican voting
majority, defense-related industrial base, active Ku Klux Klan chapter, and relative media isolation within the state. A sociologist
from Columbia University, Jay Schulman, and psychologist Richard
Christie, in working for the defense, carried out in-depth telephone
interviews in the community at different stages in an effort to construct a profile of the type of jurors most likely to support the defense of Father Philip Berrigan, Sister McAlister, and others.[25]
On the basis of their surveys the social scientists recommended
selecting for the jury young people opposed to the Vietnam War, and
working-class Lutherans, Roman Catholics, and Brethren. These
efforts were instrumental in the decision declaring a mistrial in the
case. Schulman and Christie were also influential in decisions to
drop charges in two other cases--against the Camden 28 for a draft
office raid, and against the Gainesville eight for protests by Vietnam
Veterans Against the War.[26] Pretrial research and courtroom
screening assisted in the acquittal of Attica prison inmates.[27]
Psychological research also aided in the acquittal of Angela Davis.[28]

The spring 1974 trial of Mitchell and Stans in New York City
was aided by a Long Island communications expert, Marty Herbst.[29]
These former Nixon cabinet members were charged with conspiracy,
obstructing justice, and perjury in connection with a securities investigation. On the basis of 500 interviews Herbst developed a profile of the jurors most likely to support the defense in a city where
the publicity weighed heavily against the defendants. Herbst recommended that New Yorkers selected for the jury have incomes between
$8,000 and $10,000, be working class, high school educated, Catholics, and readers of the New York Daily News rather than the New
York Post or the New York Times. These characteristics described
citizens who were home centered and had conservative political views.
The 12 jurors selected acquitted both Mitchell and Stans of the government's charges.

In the Wounded Knee trial in St. Paul in 1974 the Schulman-Christie team conducted a survey similar to that in Harrisburg.[30] The defense counsel believed the Indian leaders, Russell Means and Dennis Banks, would receive a fairer trial in St. Paul than in South Dakota because St. Paul is cosmopolitan and distant from the site of the takeover. In 575 phone interviews to prospective jurors whose names were on the voting list, citizens were asked about their views concerning government, business, politics, and Indians. These attitudes were correlated with age, sex, religion, and occupation to develop a list of those qualities most likely to be sympathetic to the defense. The profiles recommended that persons of German or Norwegian origin were apt to deal harshly with the defendants; college-educated jurors were seen as possibly more lenient. Age, sex, and political party were not important in St. Paul. Courtroom observations of prospective jurors were used along with the demographic survey and personal interviews with friends and neighbors of the jurors. In this case the judge, not the counsel, conducted the voir dire examination. The defense team included an Indian psychologist, a tribal medicine man, and a body-language psychologist. The defendants were acquitted of the charges brought against them.

Other cases can also be documented where pretrial surveys have been conducted. They have not always resulted in acquittal, as in the case of Dr. Kenneth Edelin, who, in February 1975, was convicted by a Boston jury of charges stemming from the death of a fetus. Edelin chose a jury trial after commissioning a $10,000 poll, which had revealed that in Suffolk County 85 percent of the prospective jurors favored abortion under some circumstances. Jury selection techniques were not successful in the conviction of national guardsmen in the controversial shooting at Kent State University in 1970. The 1976 trials of William and Emily Harris and of Patricia Hearst were lengthy and costly. The defense was looking for prospective jurors who had strong political motivations, views that might be in sympathy to their clients. However, the judge ruled that political questions were out of order. All three were found guilty of various kidnapping, robbery, and use-of-firearms charges.

The defense team for Patricia Hearst diligently pursued a strategy that it hoped would result in jurors being seated who had open minds in regard to their client and the charges against her. They looked for jurors who would not be averse to psychiatric testimony (they felt less-educated persons might be more skeptical of such), not be resentful of Hearst family wealth, not be hostile toward or sharply disapprove of the SLA and its revolutionary politics and sexual lifestyles, not be swayed by the massive pretrial publicity; and who might also be sympathetic to Miss Hearst as a kidnap victim. The defense team, led by F. Lee Bailey, employed a number

of methods of other social science survey teams that had been successful in previous political trials.[31]

THE GEOGRAPHER'S CONTRIBUTION

The position taken by the geographer working on the selection
of jurors is similar to the social science contributions described
above. For those geographers with professional and personal interests and training in the study of society and justice, the major contributions fall into four categories: determining the representative
quality of jury lists, preparing a social profile of the community,
designing and administering surveys, and, finally, analyzing the
results. All these efforts can be carried out to support the judicial
system within a community or to assist the defense or prosecution.
Results might be used to identify and select a more representative
jury and provide input into the voir dire examination.

With the political geographer's interests in electoral responses and related statistical surfaces within a community, he or
she is able to use the voter registration data to measure the variations and relate them to other socioeconomic or spatial attributes.
Should particular pockets or areas be identified where the registration levels are substantially below the community or district average, the county clerk or jury commissioner could be asked to increase the voter registration level by approved means or to utilize
other sources for identifying potential jurors.

When appropriate, the geographer might develop various
sampling methods from the list of potential jurors to illustrate how
specific social groups and areas are overrepresented or underrepresented by the use of a random sample. The advantages and disad-
vantages of stratified samples, socially and spatially constructed,
need to be recognized in order to determine how their use may lead
to bias or discrimination by those selected for jury duty.

With geographers' interests in the social patterns within a
city or district, they would be in a position to use census and other
published data on population change, households, employment, race,
sex, religion, occupation, and voting patterns to prepare a social
geography of the jurisdiction in question. This profile might be
based on distinct social, economic, and political clusters extracted
from a factor analysis. Mapping the areal variations on a census
tract or even block basis may assist in identifying sample areas for
subsequent interviewing. Care must be taken to insure that the
ecological fallacy is not committed. While sociologists and psychologists may perform similar exercises on the community in question,
it is the spatial character of factorial ecology models that provides

a meaningful contribution for geographers interested in social and spatial justice. On a larger scale geographers may wish to map and analyze the areal patterns in judicial caseloads, judge/population ratios, pretrial lengths, and sentencing variations. These are facets currently being investigated by various legal and governmental groups interested in the quality of justice and judicial reform.

A third contribution the social geographer can offer to legal firms and teams involves assisting in the development of the survey instrument. With training in the designing of interviewing techniques, the adoption of suitable questionnaire methods to elicit attitudes, such as the semantic differential, and experience in constructing various sampling frames, a social geographer would be able to select areas that will provide a representative cross section of a community for a jury and to supervise survey teams within the community. These data could be gathered either by telephone or by personal interviews to identify how and where community attitudes vary. The entire research design and effort would be a logical extension of the contribution geography has already made in the two steps described previously.

A fourth contribution would be in the analysis of both the aggregate and the survey data. The survey data are more important as they would form the basis for the community profiles that describe the qualities of potential jurors sympathetic to the defense or prosecution. Correlation and regression models may be used to measure the impact of sex, age, education, occupation, nationality, length of residence, political party, and religion on individual attitudes about political activism, public trust, government actions, environmental quality, specific criminal acts, minority groups, or local law enforcement. For example, through a series of statistical analyses, the profile that might emerge in a trial involving executives of a chemical company, charged with dumping solid waste materials into interstate waters, is that married women between 35 and 50 years of age who are college educated, Democrats, watch daytime television, and were raised on middle western farms are most likely to recommend conviction.

Social geographers trained in urban ecology, multivariate techniques, research design, and social psychology are in a position to have their cartographic, quantitative, and survey skills used by trial lawyers or by the courts themselves. Their contributions can be utilized in cases involving class-action suits against water pollution by nuclear power companies, or against school boards for promoting racial segregation; or in individual suits against automobile manufacturers for poor and unsafe compact-car design, against condominium developers for shoddy construction, or against airports for excess noise pollution in surrounding suburbs. Four

possible cases are described below, along with the contributions
geographers might make to identify sympathetic attitudes from community surveys.

A Jewish surgeon in a middle western city is charged with im-
properly diagnosing the extent of an injury to a star high school football player, and with performing unwarranted surgery that left the
young man paralyzed from the waist down. In this malpractice suit
the plaintiff is requesting $2 million in damages. The doctor and
his legal firm have agreed to employ a team of social scientists, including geographers, to discover the qualities of those jurors likely
to be sympathetic to this suit. For example: Are blacks more sympathetic than whites toward malpractice suits of this nature? Are
black male athletes more likely to support the doctor's defense than
black female athletes are? Are there any differences between those
jurors who have children attending biracial schools and those who
have children on athletic teams? Are there any differences between
Catholics and Protestants on welfare with respect to this case? Do
those jurors who visit their doctor at least four times a year have
different attitudes than those who pay visits only once or twice a
year? Are working-class men and women who have group hospital
plans more likely to sympathize with the doctor's defense? Do liberal Democrats who prefer football to tennis have different attitudes
than conservative Republicans have? Are college-educated women
more likely to support the doctor or the football player?
A local drive-in movie theater operator in a southern city is
charged with showing sexually explicit and obscene movies in violation of a local ordinance. The defense counsel is questioning the
legality of the statute. Are women with a high school education more
likely to recommend acquittal than men? Are there differences between jurors raised in the South and those from the East? Are mod-
erate Democrats more likely to support the defense claims than mod-
erate Republicans are? Do Baptists have different views on the issue
than Presbyterians and Methodists have? Are parents with children
in high school and college likely to recommend acquittal? Are blacks
more sympathetic than whites toward the showing of such movies?
Are the readers of Time and Newsweek more likely to recommend
acquittal than those who read Reader's Digest and National Geographic?
A land speculator in a southwestern state is charged with selling fraudulent and defective contracts for residential property. The
prosecution is attempting to select jurors he thinks will recommend
conviction. Are jurors with a rural background more likely to support his case than those raised in a large city? Are middle westerners more likely to recommend conviction than westerners and

southerners are? Do property owners have different views on this
issue than nonproperty owners have? Do residents of the community
over 55 have different attitudes than those over 45 have? Are recent
migrants into the community more likely to support the prosecution
than those who have lived there over five years? Are political liberals different from conservatives in their views? Do those families with more than two cars have different views than those with
only one? Does having a savings account instead of money in stocks
affect the individual's view on land sales?

An unwed poor white alien mother of 19 in an eastern city is
charged with starving her four-month-old baby to death. Her defense counsel is attempting to construct a profile of jurors she feels
would be most sympathetic to her case. She wants to know if mothers
in high-income neighborhoods have different attitudes than those in
low-income areas. Do divorced mothers and welfare mothers have
different views? Are low-income Catholics more likely to support
her case than rich Catholics are? Do political liberals and conservatives think alike on this issue? Do jurors who had a strict
parental upbringing have different views than those with permissive
parents? Do college-educated men behave like high school-educated
men? Do women who watch soap operas have different views than
third-generation Americans have?

In each case many of the questions posed can be answered by a
social geographer who has interest and training in urban areas,
sociology, psychology, and the appropriate sampling and analytical
techniques needed to extract the community attitudes that are likely
to be sympathetic to the defense or prosecution. Many queries relate to family background, socioeconomic status, political ideology
and affiliation, voluntary associations and hobby interests, media
influence, and attitudes toward government, authority, social change,
and groups within the community. Preparing maps and analyzing
specific social and economic characteristics, evaluating the representative nature of the voter registration or other lists, and measuring the strengths of correlations involving social and spatial data are
useful inputs geographers can contribute to trial attorneys and the
court system.

SPATIAL MODELS OF JURY SELECTION

In order to illustrate graphically the representative nature of
a jury in a hypothetical court district, two models are developed below. The residential location of the juror selected is compared with
major social patterns. Of the many possible social and behavioral

measures that could be considered, four are identified: age, income, voting preference, and race/ethnicity. The percent of the population within specific classes in each of these four categories is given, as well as the geographical area covered by each class. The figures for the district population can then be compared with the number of jurors from each area to determine whether the latter are in similar proportion to the overall district population (see Fig. 3.1).

In the first model, we will assume that the 12 jurors have been selected for duty without the use of any specific jury selection strategy by either the defense or prosecution. When the residential location of the jurors is plotted on a map of our hypothetical court district, a random pattern results (model A). However, when the residential locations are compared with particular social patterns within the district, it is found that the jury is not representative. It has more young middle-income members, more Republicans, and more residents of Anglo-Saxon background than would be expected from a true cross section. If a jury were truly representative, it would be comprised predominantly of middle-aged, middle-income persons and Anglo-Saxon Democrats. The lack of similarity between the district population and the jurors seated for a hypothetical trial lies in the procedures used to select jurors. If the presiding judge or the defense or prosecution teams were interested in seeing a representative cross section of the district on a jury, they would compare the proportion of jurors selected with varied data on major social areas within the district.

Plotting the residential locations of prospective or actual jurors on maps depicting age, income, voting, or racial/ethnic background, or other social criteria from the census or surveys, does not suggest that the individual jurors are representative of the social areas or behave according to the ecological patterns identified. The objective in comparing individual residential locations with aggregate group characteristics is only useful in measuring the degree of comparison of the jurors with overall district values and major social patterns.

In our second model (model B) let us assume that the jury depicted in model A is contested by the defense attorneys because it is socially and geographically biased. They argue that it would be impossible for their client to receive a fair trial because the members selected for jury duty were not a valid cross section of the district as a whole. Rather than preferring a biased jury, they prefer one that is representative. In their attempt to influence the selection of a fair jury, the defense team, with the aid of social geographers and other social scientists, conducted pretrial interviews in the district to ascertain the kinds of jurors likely to be sympathetic to their client and his cause. By careful screening of many prospective

MODELS OF JURY SELECTION
Residential Locations and Social Areas
in Hypothetical Court Districts

A. At Random

B. After Pre-trial Interviews

Age

Income

Age

Income

% Dist. Pop.		Jury
Old	10	1
Middle	50	3
Young	40	8

% Dist. Pop.		Jury
High	15	3
Middle	55	8
Low	30	1

% Dist. Pop.		Jury
Old	10	1
Middle	50	6
Young	40	5

% Dist. Pop.		Jury
High	15	2
Middle	55	6
Low	30	4

Voting

Race/Ethnicity

Voting

Race/Ethnicity

% Dist. Pop.		Jury
Dem.	55	3
Rep.	45	9

% Dist. Pop.		Jury
Black	15	1
E. Eur. Ethnic	40	3
Anglo-Saxon	45	8

% Dist Pop		Jury
Dem.	55	6
Rep.	45	6

% Dist. Pop.		Jury
Black	15	2
E. Eur. Ethnic	40	5
Anglo-Saxon	45	5

○ Residential Location of Juror

Source: Stanley D. Brunn, "Jury Selection, Justice, and Geography," Pennsylvania Geographer 13, no. 3 (1975): 29.

48

jurors and by using survey results, the defense team was able to
identify 12 sympathetic yet unbiased jurors who, when considered as
a whole, represented a true cross section of the district (model B).
Thus the defense felt satisfied that the criterion of a fair and representative jury had been met.

Whether the jurors selected in models A or B, or any other
model that might be developed, would come forward with a verdict
in support of the defense or of the prosecution would depend on the
evidence and arguments presented by each side. These are but two
of many models that the defense or prosecution might develop as
part of their strategy. Models could be designed to insure a valid
cross section of the district or to display bias against specific age,
income, religious, occupation, political, or racial/ethnic groups.
A jury may be dismissed, in the case of model A, because it is
shown to be unrepresentative of the district both socially and geographically. This would be a more difficult argument to refute in
the case of model B.

JUSTICE REDEFINED?

With the input geographers and other social scientists can provide in jury selection, the question arises whether justice is being
administered impartially.[32] To date, social scientists have had an
impact in helping the defense counsel obtain acquittals or mistrials
in cases involving political activists or prominent and wealthy individuals. When only the wealthy or persons with unpopular causes
can afford the assistance of social scientists to prepare community
profiles, while low- and middle-income clients cannot, it seems
that equal justice is being denied. It is important to remember that
both the prosecuting and defense attorneys use outside information
about prospective jurors in their courtroom examinations. Many
prosecutors have access to police and, often, FBI records about individuals, so the development of a profile should facilitate their efforts to seat a sympathetic jury.

Should both the defense and prosecution employ social scientists to determine the representativeness of a jury and to assist
them in their selection of jurors, it is felt the cause of justice will
be served better. Various statistical models have been developed
to aid jury selection.[33] The profiles and statistical results derived
from surveys are not in themselves decisive in the weighing of the
evidence; they only predict probable behaviors by those jurors with
certain characteristics and attitudes. Jurors and judges themselves
will be asked to weigh the evidence marshaled by social scientists;
evaluating such evidence will probably not always be easy.[34] Inasmuch

as the jury is to be a representative cross section of the community, it seems that using census and other public data as well as survey information about community attitudes is essential to determine whether the composition of a jury and the attitudes of its members reflect a fair picture of the community.

Now it appears that only those with sufficient wealth to hire social scientists for survey research and computer analysis, or those individuals with causes popular enough to enlist volunteer support, are utilizing the research efforts of sociologists, psychologists, and others. The National Jury Project is a group pioneering in this field. The time may arrive when social scientists, geographers among them, will be employed by legal firms and governments to assess community attitudes toward pending cases and determine the composition of a jury with respect to the community. In this manner the public would benefit, by having a more representative cross section of qualified individuals selected by both the defense and prosecuting attorneys to weigh the personalities, issues, and charges involved in a case. This procedure would diminish the likelihood of challenges calling a jury unrepresentative, socially and geographically, of the community.

NOTES

1. Some recent statements on this development are Amitai Etzioni, "Tampering with Juries," Current 166 (October 1974): 27-29; Deborah Shapley, "Jury Selection: Social Scientists Gamble in an Already Loaded Game," Science 185 (September 20, 1974): 1033-34; and C. Robert Zelnick, "Programmed for Acquittals? Jury Selection Techniques Queried," Christian Science Monitor, July 1, 1974, p. 3. The impact of political trials on American society and the judicial system is measured in Judith Frutig, "Political Trials: What Impact on America?" Christian Science Monitor, August 27, 1976, pp. 16-17.

2. James Kahn, "Picking Peers: Social Scientists' Role in Selection of Juries Sparks Legal Debate," Wall Street Journal, April 24, 1974, pp. 1, 19.

3. See Keith D. Harries, The Geography of Crime and Justice (New York: McGraw-Hill, 1974), pp. 89-114, and Stanley D. Brunn, Geography and Politics in America (New York: Harper and Row, 1974), pp. 199-236.

4. Benjamin S. Mackoff, "Jury Selection for the Seventies," Judicature 55 (1971): 100-04; Edward N. Beiser, "Are Juries Representative?" Judicature 57 (1973): 194-99; William J. Zumwalt, "The Anarchy of Sentencing in the Federal Courts," Judicature 57 (1973): 96-104.

5. David Harvey, Social Justice and the City (Baltimore: Johns Hopkins Press, 1973), pp. 96-118.

6. A number of strategies are discussed in William J. Bryan, Jr., The Chosen Ones or the Psychology of Jury Selection (New York: Vantage Press, 1971).

7. Kahn, op. cit.

8. Marcus Gleisser, Juries and Justice (New York: A. S. Barnes, 1968), pp. 235-41.

9. Angus Campbell et al., The American Voter (New York: Wiley, 1964).

10. Beiser, op. cit.

11. "Suit Alleges Bias in Picking Grand Juries in Queens," New York Times, August 7, 1973, p. 27.

12. Tom Goldstein, "State Court Says Jury Selection on S. I. Is 'Irremediably Tainted,'" New York Times, November 10, 1976, pp. 1, 13, and Max Seigel, "Judicial Dispute Affects Makeup of Juries on S. I.," New York Times, March 6, 1977, p. 45.

13. "Denver Judge Disqualifies Jurors as Being Too Old," New York Times, January 10, 1971, p. 51.

14. "High Court Sees Jury Bias Against Group That Is Governing Majority," New York Times, March 24, 1977, p. 19.

15. "The Exclusion of Young Adults from Juries: A Threat to Jury Impartiality," Journal of Criminal Law and Criminology 66 (1975): 150-64.

16. Iver Peterson, "Court Reform Measures Moving Ahead in Albany," New York Times, June 23, 1976, p. 42.

17. Bryan, op. cit., p. 73.

18. Curtis J. Sitomer, "Making Jury Duty Mandatory, Better Paying," Christian Science Monitor, February 25, 1976, p. 6.

19. Views of citizens regarding jury duty are expressed in E. Patrick Healy, "Memoirs of a Manhattan Juror: An Adventure in Apathy," American Bar Association Journal 62 (1976): 460-63; W. R. Pabst, Jr. et al., "Myth of the Unwilling Juror," Judicature 60 (1976): 164-71; Caroline K. Simon, "The Juror in New York City: Attitudes and Experiences," American Bar Association Journal 61 (1975): 207-11.

20. "U.S. Judge Invalidates System of Sentencing Juries in Alabama," New York Times, June 10, 1973, p. 51.

21. "Conviction Reversed," New York Times, June 10, 1973, p. 51.

22. American Bar Association, Institute for Judicial Administration, Special Committee on Minimum Standards for the Administration of Criminal Justice, Standards Relating to Trial by Jury (Chicago: American Bar Association, 1968), pp. 63-67.

23. Harry L. Hannah, "Voir Dire: Its Value--How to Use It," Judicature 55 (1971): 110-15; Alice M. Padawer-Singer et al., "Voir Dire by Two Lawyers: An Essential Safeguard," Judicature 57 (1974): 386-91; Barbara A. Babcock, "Voir Dire: Preserving 'Its Wonderful Power,'" Stanford Law Review 27 (1975): 545-65.

24. A number of demographic and behavioral characteristics are treated in Cookie Stephan, "Selective Characteristics of Jurors and Litigants: Their Influence on Juries' Verdicts," in The Jury System in America, ed. Rita James Simon (Beverly Hills: Sage Publications, 1975), pp. 95-121.

25. Jay Schulman et al., "Recipe for a Jury," Psychology Today 6, no. 12 (1973): 37-49.

26. "Judging Jurors," Time, January 28, 1974, p. 60.

27. Paul G. Chevigny, "The Attica Cases: A Successful Jury Challenge in a Northern City [Buffalo, N.Y. and environs]," Criminal Law Bulletin 11 (1975): 157-72. The biased selection procedures used in Erie County, New York, are critically evaluated in Adeline G. Levine and Claudine Schweber-Koren, "Jury Selection in Erie County: Changing a Sexist System," Law and Society Review 11 (1976): 43-56.

28. Louis Robinson, "How Psychology Helped Free Angela Davis," Ebony, February 1973, pp. 44-46.

29. Kahn, op. cit., and Hans Zeisel and Seidman Diamond, "The Jury Selection in the Mitchell-Stans Conspiracy Trial," American Bar Foundation Research Journal 1 (1976): 151-64.

30. "Finding a Friendly Jury," Newsweek, August 26, 1974, pp. 49-50.

31. Frederic A. Moritz, "How Hearst Jury Is Being Selected," Christian Science Monitor, January 30, 1976, p. 3.

32. "The Fairness Factor," Time, March 18, 1974, p. 71.

33. Michael Fried et al., "Juror Selection: An Analysis of Voir Dire," in The Jury System in America, op. cit., pp. 47-66. Other nonspatial models that are useful have been developed in Howard R. Alker, Jr. et al., "Jury Selection as a Biased Social Process," Law and Society Review 11 (1976): 9-42, which identifies biases that exist in the system and recommends procedures to reduce it, and in David Kairys, "Juror Selection: The Law, A Mathematical Method of Analysis and a Case Study," American Criminal Law Review 10 (1972): 771.

34. The question is raised with respect to judges in Roger Handberg, "Can Judges Evaluate Social Science Evidence?" Judicature 60 (1977): 362-63.

4

SENTENCE DISPARITY:
APPROACHES TO
EXPLANATION

Sentence disparity is an aspect of the administration of justice that has been receiving substantial attention in recent years. This attention has run the gamut from television and the printed media, to popular books, and more academic treatments in books and journals.[1] The National Advisory Commission on Criminal Justice Standards and Goals pointed to the impact of sentence disparity in the correctional process, citing it as a "source of offender resentment that makes the correctional task more difficult."[2] Senator Edward Kennedy referred to "the sentencing lottery in our nation's courtrooms" in an appeal for reform of sentencing practices at the federal level.[3]

The critics generally avoid the accusation that all disparity is undesirable--what is attacked is unjustified or unexplained disparity in cases involving similar defendants and similar crimes. Indeterminate sentencing, which involves sentencing of offenders to indefinite periods of confinement--say, 5 to 20 years--necessarily means the exercise of enormous discretion. This discretion is exercised by the judge when, in sentencing, he uses the legislatively set range, and by parole boards that ultimately determine the precise fate of the offender.[4] In such a system (which is currently under great pressure for reform), discretion all too easily becomes disparity. The President's Commission on Law Enforcement and Administration of Justice described disparity as "a pervasive problem in almost all jurisdictions," one which "may reflect geographic factors, such as differences in public apprehension of crime among communities in the same jurisdiction. . . ."[5] Kenneth Davis has likened legal research to repairing a roof--the legal "roof" is strong at the rules end, but rotten at the discretion end, "leaving big holes where the water rushes in and does great damage." Furthermore, he said, "the power of judges to sentence criminal defendants is one of the best examples of unstructured discretionary power that can and should be structured. The degree of disparity from one judge to another is widely regarded as a disgrace to the legal system."[6]

The Committee for the Study of Incarceration has similarly condemned the unrestrained discretion that is practiced in the name of "individualization" of sentences. Among its proposed reforms are reduction of sentence disparity and the exercising of sentencing discretion (in part through the use of "presumptive" sentences), and the elimination of indeterminate sentencing.[7] Even the criminal justice establishment recognizes the existence of the problem:

> Fairness demands that two individuals convicted of the same offense, with similar backgrounds and criminal histories, should receive sentences that are roughly the same. Nevertheless, extreme disparities in sentencing are commonplace; . . . research in Chicago and New York has shown, for example, that three judges, given the same case to sentence, will disagree on the basic issue of whether or not to imprison approximately 30 per cent of the time. When such disparities abound, public confidence in criminal justice is undermined.[8]

Chief Justice Warren Burger approached the issue delicately: "Discretion in sentencing has been a double-edged sword. It permits the judge to accommodate unusual circumstances relative to each defendant. But this sometimes results in defendants who ought to be similarly treated receiving substantially disparate sentences."[9]

Among the most comprehensive recent reviews of the problem of sentencing bias are those by Marvin Frankel and Willard Gaylin; Frankel's treatment is probably the single most widely quoted source, and no attempt will be made to review it here. Suffice it to say that Frankel not only discusses the problem in abstract terms, but is also able to spice his discussion with chilling examples of abuses of discretion, and of other sources of sentencing inequity: "breaking into a car to steal from its glove compartment could result in up to fifteen years in California, while stealing the entire car carried a maximum of ten."[10]

Gaylin's treatment is equally convincing. He pays attention to geographic inequities:

> When I pursued the question of sentencing with the war resisters, the disparity seemed appalling and

unbelievable. The cruelty of chance (in these
cases, geography was a primary factor) created
inequities that should be unthinkable in a reasonable society. In Oregon, of thirty-three convicted Selective Service violators, eighteen were
put on probation; in southern Texas, of sixteen
violators, none were put on probation. In Oregon,
not a single man was given a sentence of over
three years; in southern Texas, fifteen out of
sixteen were given over three-year sentences--
fourteen were given the five-year maximum
allowable by law. In southern Mississippi,
every defendant was convicted, and everyone
was given the maximum of five years.

Geographical differences in sentencing within
the United States seem particularly offensive when
involving federal crimes, since by definition the
crime is seen to be one against the nation as a
whole. [11]

The Selective Service example selected by Gaylin is a particularly good one. Analysis of such cases, using 1972 data, shows that
the California Northern federal court district, centered in San
Francisco, commenced 661 cases, or 12.9 percent of the national
total, while accommodating only 2.5 percent of the nation's population. The Ninth Circuit (western states) commenced Selective Service cases at the rate of 52.5 per million, compared to 10 per
million in the First Circuit (northeastern states). [12] The personal
passions of judges vis-a-vis patriotism, obligations of young men
to their country, and so forth, found easy expression in sentencing
discretion in connection with Selective Service cases. It appears
that sentence severity was linked with almost stereotypical regularity
to the philosophies of federal judges, which, more often than not,
reflected the preferences of their districts. [13] Examples of sentence
disparity in federal and state courts are presented in Chapter 6, and
the theme will not be amplified here; critical reviews and examples
of sentencing problems are too numerous to discuss, and such a review would only belabor the point that disparity is an extremely
serious issue, and a well-documented one. [14]

This chapter, and the two that follow, emphasize the geographical dimension of the sentencing process--the idea that variations in
sentencing are not random occurrences from court district to court
district, but that certain systematic influences affect sentencing
outcomes in a particular manner, from which regionally disparate
treatment of similar offenders and offenses may reasonably be

inferred. The existence of such spatial disparity is not in question
--the phenomenon was discussed at length by Gaylin and has been
recognized in a more formal roster of research priorities in sentencing. [15]

That sentence disparity may have numerous possible sources
is obvious. What is less obvious is precisely what those sources
are, and which, if any, may be expected to manifest, or contribute
to, spatial variation. The balance of this chapter is devoted to a
discussion of possible causes, usually referred to as independent
variables. In Chapter 5, the role of the prosecutor is singled out
for special attention; in Chapter 6, the focus is on district-to-
district sentencing variations in several geographic contexts.

INDEPENDENT VARIABLES

A genuinely thorough search for causes of sentence disparity
would soon get out of hand--we would be forced to investigate the
idiosyncrasies of private lives of judges and prosecutors, and to
practice remote psychoanalysis on members of pardon and parole
boards. The intent here is to paint with a broader brush, to suggest the main classes of independent variables upon which concern
should focus, with particular emphasis on those that may contribute
appreciably to geographic inconsistencies; variables relating to
crime-rate differentials are therefore excluded from discussion on
the ground that differences in crime seriousness actually justify
disparity. In a more general sense, the emphasis will be on variables that are legally irrelevant--not because disparity cannot
originate in legally relevant conditions, but rather because such
disparity is more readily justified. Prior record, for example,
typically emerges as a significant explanatory variable in the sentencing process, and such a relationship is theoretically justifiable
(see Table 6.2 for the influence of prior record in a sentencing
model). A judge may overreact or underreact to the prior record
of a given defendant and thus contribute to sentence disparity; however, disparity based on legally relevant factors is less objection-
able than disparity traceable to entirely irrelevant considerations
such as race or sex.

One class of essentially legally irrelevant variables relates
to the structures of the legal system and of the sentencing process.
These include "legislative inaction or inattention to sentencing
statutes," "lack of communication among judges concerning the
goals and desiderata of sentencing," "lack of communication between
sentencing courts and the correctional system," the lack of famil-
iarity of judges with the institutions to which offenders are sentenced,

and "lack of information about available sentencing alternatives."[16] In the sense that these causes of disparity are likely to occur in rather uniform fashion across any given system, they will not be likely to contribute to spatial disparity, and will not be further discussed.

Variables that do have considerable potential for contributing to interdistrict variations may be divided into three broad categories, which will be reviewed in turn: the characteristics of the court, which is interpreted here to include the prosecutor, judge, and jury; the characteristics of the defendant, including race, sex, age, and economic status; the cultural milieu.

The Court

Several court-related conditions may have profound effects on sentencing. The best-concealed of these is the posture of the district attorney, or prosecutor. The traditional assumption has been that sentence disparity is attributable solely to judges--in part, perhaps, because the judge makes a public pronouncement of sentence. However, much of the real work of sentencing is done not in public by the judge, but in private by the prosecutor in conjunction with the defense attorney. It is no secret that prosecutors often use their offices as a basis for political haymaking, in order to step up to higher elected offices; the combination of secrecy and playing to the gallery lends itself to arbitrary treatment of defendants and may contribute to serious disparity within and between districts. The role of the prosecutor is important enough and neglected enough to warrant separate treatment, which is given in Chapter 5. The Oklahoma drug sentencing example in Chapter 6 also lends weight to the argument that prosecutorial discretion has historically been underestimated in its influence on sentencing. The prosecutor may further contribute to disparity between districts by promoting hard or soft approaches to sentencing in comparison with other districts. It is suggested in the following chapters that this may be the case in Oklahoma when Tulsa and Oklahoma Counties are compared.

The role of juries in sentencing is relatively limited. In 1973, only 13 states still allowed jury sentencing in noncapital cases:

> . . . the practice has been condemned by every
> serious study and analysis of sentencing in the
> last half-century. Jury sentencing is arbitrary,
> nonprofessional, and based more often on emo-
> tions arising from the offense or the offender
> than on needs of the offender or available

resources of the correctional system. Sentencing by jury leads to grossly disparate sentences
without effective means of control and leaves
little latitude for development of sentencing
policies.[17]

While very few cases are actually sentenced by juries, analysis
does suggest that juries are indeed capricious and severe (see Table
6.7). However, as an independent variable, jury sentencing does
not appear to contribute to geographic variability; jury influence
seems to be exercised randomly, so that sentences imposed by
juries do not vary significantly between districts, at least insofar
as the limited analysis indicates.

Considerable attention has been given to the role of judges in
sentencing, and there is a substantial literature, mainly in political
science, on the relationship between judicial characteristics and
behavior. Some of these characteristics are amplified and documented in the discussion of federal sentencing in Chapter 6. It is
suggested that such factors as age, political philosophy, culture
area of education and/or upbringing, and religious preference are
likely to impact on judicial attitudes with respect to leniency and
punitiveness. A militaristic judge, for example, may have been
more likely to punish Selective Service offenders severely, as compared to a pacifist judge, during the period of compulsory induction.

In a study of ten Texas criminal court districts in Harris
County in 1970, James Johnson looked at the relationship between
27 judicial characteristics and sentencing records. The judicial
traits included measures of personal background, professional
career and judicial attitudes. Although there were statistically
significant deviations in sentences among similar cases, it was concluded that "the backgrounds and attitudes of the judges explain very
few of the sentencing deviations found to exist in the criminal district courts of Harris County."[18]

Somewhat contradictory findings emerged from a study of sentencing by 55 magistrates in the English Midlands. These unpaid
jurists were found to be influenced in their sentencing by variables
including training, experience, and attitudes toward law and punishment.[19] A landmark U.S. study of sentencing in the federal courts
denied the influence of experience that was revealed by the English
study.[20] However, the contexts are not comparable; federal judges
have a legal background while English magistrates are nonprofes-
sionals. These conflicting findings are symptomatic of the difficul-
ties involved in analyses of judicial characteristics. The U.S.
Second Circuit study cited above is particularly important because
it was a sentencing experiment, in the sense that judges rendered

sentences for hypothetical cases under controlled conditions. But characteristics of judges, apart from experience, were not included in the study, which focused, rather, on case characteristics. It was pointed out that "relative to one another, individual judges appear sometimes lenient and sometimes severe."[21]

The fact that there is substantial intradistrict sentencing variation attributable solely to judges does little to encourage the use of judicial characteristics as independent variables for developing an explanation of interdistrict variation. As noted in the Second Circuit analysis, each judge's own disparities are often self-canceling in a statistical sense--one would have to develop fine taxonomic detail in order to find classes of offenses to which individual judges might react with consistent harshness or leniency. Even then, the statistical effects of aggregating judges by district are likely to be self-canceling.

Other court-related variables have been identified as contributors to disparity: quality of the defense counsel and his knowledge of plea bargaining, searching for a judge to handle a particular case, and delaying tactics; the probation officer and his attitude toward the defendant; the volume of court business; and "other factors which significantly affect the outcome in a criminal case."[22] The latter could include the type of plea, mode of trial (judge or jury), and time lapse to disposition of case, to identify a few examples.

In reality, then, despite its superficial simplicity, the sentencing process is an extremely complex mix of attitudes, events, and outcomes, even when one considers only court-related sources of variation. The complexity increases when the person being sentenced is included in the equation.

Characteristics of the Defendant

The attributes of defendants may, from certain perspectives, be regarded as either legally relevant or irrelevant. Since the emphasis here is on the legally irrelevant, defendant characteristics should be treated circumspectly--sentencing bias can rightly be attributed to such characteristics only after controlling (at least) the statistical effects of the seriousness of the crimes committed. In 1975, for example, 54.4 percent of all homicide arrests were of blacks, who presumably generally attracted severe sentences.[23] But it is unrealistic to regard this disproportionate allocation of severity to blacks as sentence disparity. The criminal justice system is essentially operating rationally in dealing most harshly with the most severe offenders. The disparity lies, rather, in factors of the social and cultural milieu contributing to the high homicide rates

among blacks, or in the attitudes defining black crimes differently
from those of whites. [24]

In past studies, numerous defendant-related variables have
been cited as contributors to sentence disparity. For the purposes
of this discussion, such variables may be regarded as descriptive
of race, age, sex, and socioeconomic status (SES). Other measures
that have been reviewed in other studies have included employment
status (which may be subsumed under SES), type of offense, prompt-
ness of arrest, bail status, prior record, and attorney status. [25]
Some studies have considered victim characteristics on the ground
that higher-status or more vulnerable victims will attract harsher
sentences.

Race

The question of the relationship between sentence severity and
race has attracted much attention, and the classic studies are probably those of Henry Bullock and Edward Green. Bullock analyzed
data for 3,644 Texas prisoners and assigned them to various dichot-
omies including long and short sentences. Both racial and nonracial
factors appeared to relate to sentence length, including guilty pleas
and, of particular relevance in this discussion, region. Bullock
distinguished between eastern and western Texas and found that long
sentences were meted out significantly more frequently in the former
than in the latter region. Also, metropolitan counties were significantly more severe than rural (a similar dichotomy is used in Chapter 6 to test for regional effects in district court sentencing in
Oklahoma). When nonracial factors were controlled, Bullock found
the degree of association between race and sentence length increased:
"'being black' generally means one type of sentence while 'being
white' means another." Blacks received shorter sentences for
murder and rape, as compared to whites, but longer sentences for
burglary. Sentence length related to whether crimes were inter-
racial or intraracial, with the latter attracting relatively lenient
sentences and thereby prompting Bullock to point out that sentencing
patterns may be regarded as "indulgent" and "non-indulgent." He
concluded: "Those who enforce the law conform to the norms of
their local society concerning racial prejudice, thus denying equality
before the law. That criminal statistics reflect social customs,
values, and prejudices appears to be further validated. "[26]

Green, on the other hand, asserted that there was "no warrant
for the charge of racial discrimination in sentencing." He found
variation in sentencing, but saw it as "a function of intrinsic differences between the races in patterns of criminal behavior"; that is,
within a given crime category, blacks are more likely than whites to

have committed "aggravated" offenses, which would rationally attract more severe sentences.[27] This assertion would seem to be
confounded by the phenomena of overcharging and overarresting
blacks, particularly in some southern culture areas. Thus a black
and a white who commit physically identical acts may be charged
and sentenced differentially, creating an appearance of equality before the law, which is obviously fallacious.

Carl Pope, in one of his California sentencing monographs, has
reviewed some of the contradictory findings relating to the role of
race in sentencing; he makes the point that data inadequacy has probably been a key problem in explaining the inconsistency of analytical
results.[28]

Age and Sex

A federal study of defendant characteristics has shown that
age did not relate to type of sentence, but did relate to length when
the prior-record factor was controlled. Defendants in the under-21
cohort received relatively short sentences, and there was a consistently positive relationship between sentence severity and age. With
respect to sex, it was found that over 90 percent of all defendants
were men, and that the mean prison percent for men were about
twice those of women, across the nation. The sentence lengths of
males were, on the average, always higher than those for females,
but not significantly so.[29] However, in a comprehensive review of
the socioeconomic and demographic correlates of sentencing, John
Hagan concluded that age makes a small contribution to the sentencing decision, while sex has a "negligible" role when offense type and
prior record are controlled factors.[30] As is the case with other
variables, further conflicting evidence is readily available. Pope
found that in California superior courts females often served less
time than males (when prior record was controlled), with greater
urban than rural differences indicated. Also in superior court,
younger offenders were less likely to receive severe sentences, as
compared to older ones, when prior criminal history was controlled.[31]

Socioeconomic Status

Hagan's review points to differences in the influence of SES
according to the types of cases involved. In federal larceny cases,
holding legally relevant variables constant, "knowledge of social
class increases accuracy in predicting the sentencing decision by
less than one percent." In capital cases, the influence of SES appeared to be a little stronger.[32] In a study of 798 burglary and
larceny defendants in Mecklenburg County, North Carolina (1971),

Stevens Clarke and Gary Koch concluded: "Other things being equal, the higher-income defendant seems more likely to emerge from the criminal court without an active prison sentence than the lower-income defendant."[33] This finding appears to be at odds with a test of the "conflict" proposition* developed by Theodore Chiricos and Gordon Waldo. They studied 10,488 inmates in three states; SES scores and some additional variables were developed for each inmate and related to sentence length. Some 185 correlations between SES and sentence length (based on varying numbers of cases [Ns]) were computed. The conflict perspective hypothesizes negative r's in this context, but only one negative r was significant, compared to ten positive r's.[34] It is possible that Chiricos and Waldo defined criminal sentencing too narrowly in using it to relate SES to sentence length. Sanctions other than imprisonment should be taken into account--it is likely that the most profound influence of SES occurs long before the stage of imprisonment, in such processes as the hiring of counsel (with its influence in plea negotiation) and bail. If SES is a factor in the processing of criminal defendants, it will surely be effective long before the penitentiary comes into view.[35]

The Cultural Milieu

In theory, the cultural environment should have a strong effect on sentencing patterns since judges in many areas are elected, and it is reasonable to expect that, once on the bench, they will be predisposed to reflect the preferences of their constituency. Bullock's point about the difference between eastern and western Texas has already been cited, and one need only look at maps of state-based rates of incarceration and execution to appreciate that there is a regional way of doing things in the United States.[36] It would be redundant to explore here all the facets of culture that may influence sentencing decisions on a regional basis--in Chapter 6 a regional model relating to Oklahoma is developed at some length, and the point to be made here is that culture may contribute to the judicial process, just as it contributes to criminogenesis.[37] It is intriguing to reflect on the fact that the law is written on the implicit assumption that there is no intrastate variation in culture--there are indeterminate sentences, but the basic framework of the law is uniform within each state, and, for federal law, within the United States. But in practice, the law has many local options, which in some

---

*Conflict theory may be reduced in its simplest terms to the notion of the power structure versus the rest.

cases represent the adaptation of the law to local mores, often with disastrous results for individuals or groups who may not happen to be in the mainstream of those mores at a particular point in time--or space.

THE SPATIAL DIMENSION

Which, if any, of the explanatory variables or conditions discussed previously can be expected to manifest significant spatial variation? There is no simple or objective explanation--in one context, one factor or a set of factors may be sources of such variation, and in another context, quite different processes may be at work. It is reasonable to suggest that at any given time any or all of the three categories of variables--court related, defendant related, and culturally related--may show up as sources of geographical disparity. But they may also cancel each other out, and reduce the usefulness of a spatial approach in certain research designs.

A descriptive statistic for a group of observations within a geographic area may be quite unrepresentative of the actual statistical distribution. Distributions of sentencing data may be polarized, for large or small geographic areas, and a mean or median may represent neither pole. This hazard of ecological analysis can affect outcomes in sentence disparity analyses; hypothesis formulation and testing may therefore yield surprising results owing to unanticipated sources of sentence variation, based on choice of variables, the shape of their statistical distributions, and levels of spatial aggregation.

It may be argued that, from a policy and management perspective, what is critical is the identification of disparity--sophisticated analyses of causes are quite impractical in most court systems. Once disparity is identified in a particular system, then resources can be brought to bear on causal analysis and elimination of the problem. Is there a general strategy, or model, of the spatial analysis of sentence disparity that might be applicable to the federal courts or to any state system of district courts? One possibility is what might be called "progressive disparity analysis," involving a search for disparity at different levels of geographic aggregation. In the first step, intradistrict variations would be identified, using individual judges--in whom is vested nominal responsibility for sentencing. Then districts within a region or regional administrative unit would be compared, with the overriding objective of seeking sentences that are significant departures from normal, or random, variation. Then regions are compared within the state as the last step in disparity identification. What complicates this model is not only the typical lack of data--a mechanical problem--but also the statistical problem that arises when it is realized that, in small-population rural counties, in particular, many felonies will not be committed in a given year or be committed in such small numbers that statistics become very unreliable. This draws attention to the importance of an historical data base to enable the development of sentence expectations for particular offenses--essentially the presumptive sentence currently advocated by some.

In practical terms, it would be unrealistic to expect that disparity research could be undertaken for all crimes. Initially, resources should focus on the most common felonies, such as burglary, and within these common offenses efforts should be concentrated primarily on offenses attracting the severest penalties.

Prosecutor's use of discretion and attitudes toward sentencing should be incorporated into a spatial model of sentencing, as should the impact of a parole board--which should ideally be expected to even up disparities in indeterminate sentences. But the parole board also has the ability to accentuate existing disparities, and the negative role of the parole system has been documented in the official account of the Attica prison disturbance in which 43 died: "inmates' criticisms were echoed by many parole officers and corrections personnel, who agreed that the operation of the parole system was a primary source of tension and bitterness within the walls."[38] Analysis of the spatial impacts of the parole process are beyond the scope of this volume, but the prosecution process and associated sentencing patterns are reviewed in the next chapter.

NOTES

1. Examples of the more popular treatments include ABC Television, "Justice on Trial," January 7, 1977; Jessica Mitford, Kind and Usual Punishment (New York: Alfred A. Knopf, 1973); "Fairer Sentences," Newsweek, April 26, 1976, p. 107; "Agnew Case Points Up Inconsistent Sentencing for Criminal Offenses," Wall Street Journal, October 26, 1973, p. 1; "Toward Equal Punishment," New York Times, March 10, 1976, p. 34.

2. National Advisory Commission on Criminal Justice Standards and Goals, Courts (Washington, D.C.: U.S. Government Printing Office, 1973), p. 6.

3. Edward M. Kennedy, "Criminal Sentencing: A Game of Chance," Judicature 60 (1976): 208-15.

4. For further discussion, see Alan M. Dershowitz, "Criminal Sentencing in the United States: An Historical and Conceptual

Overview," Annals, American Academy of Political and Social
Science 423 (1976): 130.

5. Robert W. Winslow, Crime in a Free Society: Selections
from the President's Commission on Law Enforcement and Administration of Justice (Belmont, Calif.: Dickenson Publishing, 1969),
pp. 305-06. Several examples of disparity are cited, including one
from Detroit in which one judge imprisoned 75-90 percent of defendants, and another judge, 35 percent, over a 20-month period.

6. Kenneth Culp Davis, Discretionary Justice: A Preliminary Inquiry (Baton Rouge: Louisiana State University Press, 1969),
pp. vi-vii, 133.

7. Andrew von Hirsch, Doing Justice: Report of the Committee for the Study of Incarceration (New York: Hill and Wang,
1976), pp. xvii, and 29.

8. National Institute of Law Enforcement and Criminal
Justice, Courts Research: An Overview (n.p., May 1976).

9. Chief Justice Warren E. Burger, Year-End Report
(Washington, D.C.: U.S. Supreme Court, January 2, 1977), p. 7.

10. Marvin E. Frankel, Criminal Sentences: Law Without
Order (New York: Hill and Wang, 1973), p. 9.

11. Willard Gaylin, Partial Justice: A Study of Bias in Sentencing (New York: Vintage Books, 1974), pp. 6-7.

12. Keith D. Harries, "Modeling the Geography of Justice:
Issues and Methodological Problems," Transition 6 (1976): 14-20.
See Map 7.1, which shows the federal districts and circuits.

13. This admittedly speculative view was originally encouraged by a series of personal interviews with federal judges in
Oklahoma.

14. Some examples include American Bar Association, Project on Standards for Criminal Justice, Standards Relating to Sentencing Alternatives and Procedures (New York: American Bar
Association, 1968); "Probation in Illinois," California Public Survey 24 (1972): 131; S. R. Brady, The Effectiveness of Sentencing--
A Review of the Literature (London: Her Majesty's Stationery Office, 1976), pp. 3-4; Alan M. Dershowitz, "Indeterminate Confine-
ment: Letting the Therapy Fit the Harm," University of Pennsylvania Law Review 123 (1974): 297-339; Daniel Glaser, Fred Cohen,
and Vincent O'Leary, The Sentencing and Parole Process (Washington, D.C.: U.S. Government Printing Office, 1966), pp. 3-4;
Keith D. Harries, The Geography of Crime and Justice (New York:
McGraw-Hill, 1974), Chapter 5; Chris A. Korbakes, "Criminal
Sentencing--Is the Judge's Sound Discretion Subject to Review?"
Judicature 59 (1975): 112-19; Chris A. Korbakes, "Criminal Sen-
tencing--Should the Judge's Sound Discretion Be Explained?"
Judicature 59 (1975): 184-91; Harold E. Lane, "Illogical Variations

in Sentences of Felons Committed to Massachusetts State Prison,"
Journal of Criminal Law and Criminology 32 (1974): 171-90;
Richard A. McGee, "A New Look at Sentencing," Federal Probation
38 (1974): 3-8; Larry I. Palmer, "A Model of Criminal Disposi-
tions: An Alternative to Official Discretion in Sentencing," The
Georgetown Law Journal 62 (1973): 1-59; Mark P. Rabinowitz,
"Criminal Sentencing: An Overview of Procedures and Alternatives,"
Mississippi Law Journal 45 (1974): 782-99; James Steele and
Donald Barlett, "Justice in Philadelphia," The New Republic,
May 26, 1973, pp. 19-21; Nigel Walker, Sentencing in a Rational
Society (New York: Basic Books, 1971); G. D. Woods, "Criminol-
ogy and Sentencing in the New South Wales Court of Criminal Ap-
peal," Criminal Law Review (1974): 409-14.

    15. John C. Ruhnka, Research Priorities in Sentencing
(Denver: National Center for State Courts, 1975). In this document,
the director of research of the American Judicature Society suggested several research targets; for example, "analyze regional and
individual disparity in sentencing" (p. 37).

    16. These conditions were cited as causes of disparity in
National Advisory Commission on Criminal Justice Standards and
Goals, Corrections (Washington, D.C.: U.S. Government Printing
Office, 1973), pp. 146-47.

    17. Ibid., p. 148. As a member of the Oklahoma Criminal
Justice Standards and Goals Advisory Committee, coauthor Keith
Harries proposed the abolition of jury sentencing as a formal goal.
Prosecutors and law enforcement interests voiced strong objections
("Offenders should face juries of their peers"), and the proposition
failed (Oklahoma Criminal Justice Standards and Goals Conference,
Roman Nose State Lodge, Oklahoma, March 5, 1977).

    18. James N. Johnson, "Sentencing in the Criminal District
Courts," Houston Law Review 9 (1972): 993-94.

    19. Nigel Lemon, "Training, Personality and Attitude as
Determinants of Magistrates' Sentencing," British Journal of
Criminology 14 (1974): 45-46.

    20. Anthony Partridge and William B. Eldridge, The Second
Circuit Sentencing Study (Washington, D.C.: Federal Judicial
Center, 1974), pp. 34-35.

    21. Ibid., p. 37.

    22. Judge Harold Rothwax (Criminal Court of the City of New
York), quoted in Ruhnka, op. cit., p. 20.

    23. Federal Bureau of Investigation, Uniform Crime Reports
--1975 (Washington, D.C.: U.S. Government Printing Office,
1976), Table 39, p. 192.

    24. Private conversation with Bruce Garwood, former chief
of police of Petal, Mississippi, at a crime analysis workshop,

University of Tennessee, Chattanooga (March 15, 1977). Garwood
pointed out that in Mississippi an assault by a black on a white is in
practice defined differently from an assault by a white on a black.
He described an incident in which he had to seek a grand-jury indictment of a white allegedly involved in the rape of a young black girl.
Such an indictment would not have been necessary if the races of the
participants had been reversed.

25. See, for example, Stevens H. Clarke and Gary G. Koch,
"Who Goes to Prison? The Likelihood of Receiving an Active Sentence," Popular Government 41 (1975): 29. Attorney status is
dealt with briefly in Chapters 5 and 6.

26. Henry Allen Bullock, "Significance of the Racial Factor
in the Length of Prison Sentences," Journal of Criminal Law,
Criminology, and Police Science 52 (1961): 417.

27. Edward Green, "Inter- and Intra-racial Crime Relative
to Sentencing," Journal of Criminal Law, Criminology and Police
Science 55 (1964): 358.

28. Carl E. Pope, Sentencing of California Felony Offenders
(Washington, D.C.: U.S. Government Printing Office, 1976),
pp. 10-11. Other studies focusing on the relationship between race
and sentencing include A. Didrick Castberg, "The Ethnic Factor in
Criminal Sentencing," Western Political Quarterly 24 (1971):
425-37; Alan M. Dershowitz, Fair and Certain Punishment (New
York: McGraw-Hill, 1976), pp. 105-06; Edwin L. Hall and Albert A.
Simkus, "Inequality in the Types of Sentences Received by Native
Americans and Whites," Criminology 13 (1975): 199-222; Joseph C.
Howard, "Racial Discrimination in Sentencing," Judicature 59
(1975): 121-25; Henry E. Kelly, "A Comparison of Defense Strategy
and Race as Influences in Differential Sentencing," Criminology 14
(1976): 241-49; Terence P. Thornberry, "Race, Socioeconomic
Status and Sentencing in the Juvenile Justice System," Journal of
Criminal Law and Criminology 64 (1973): 90-98; Marvin E. Wolfgang
and Marc Ridel, "Race, Judicial Discretion, and the Death Penalty,"
Annals, American Academy of Political and Social Science 407
(1973): 119-33. This last study found that "sentences of death have
been imposed on blacks, compared to whites, in a way that exceeds
any statistical notion of chance or fortuity" (p. 133).

29. U.S. Congress, Senate, Committee on the Judiciary,
Hearing before the Subcommittee on Criminal Laws and Procedures,
92d Cong., 2d sess., cited in Reform of the Federal Criminal Laws
(Washington, D.C.: U.S. Government Printing Office, 1972), pp.
3905-07.

30. John Hagan, "Extra-legal Attributes and Criminal Sentencing: An Assessment of a Sociological Viewpoint," Law and
Society Review 8 (1974): 375. For other perspectives on sex as an

independent variable, see Karen De Crow, Sexist Justice (New York: Vintage Books, 1975), and Stuart Nagel and Lenore J. Weitzman, "Double Standard of American Justice," Society 9 (1972): 18-25, 62-63.

31. Pope, op. cit., pp. 24-26.

32. Hagan, op. cit., pp. 373-74.

33. Clarke and Koch, op. cit., p. 33.

34. Theodore G. Chiricos and Gordon P. Waldo, "Socioeconomic Status and Criminal Sentencing: An Empirical Assessment of a Conflict Proposition," American Sociological Review 40 (1975): 753-72.

35. This is essentially the argument developed in Clarke and Koch, op. cit.

36. See U.S. Department of Justice, National Criminal Justice Information and Statistics Service, Capital Punishment, 1975 (Washington, D.C.: U.S. Government Printing Office, 1976), and U.S. Department of Justice, National Criminal Justice Information and Statistics Service, Prisoners in State and Federal Institutions on December 3, 1974 (Washington, D.C.: U.S. Government Printing Office, 1976). D. A. Thomas has provided interesting examples of the impact of local culture on sentencing in England. A Westmoreland County sheep farmer appealed a three-year sentence for the larceny of sheep and lambs. The appeal was rejected because of the importance of trust in that region, where pastures are unfenced. In Lincolnshire, 18 girls and 40 boys were convicted of engaging in sexual adventures; on appeal their sentences were upheld because of the "wholesale scale of the activity," which meant that "something in the nature of a deterrent sentence is clearly called for." This was seen as a local problem calling for exemplary strictness in sentencing. See Thomas, Principles of Sentencing: The Sentencing Policy of the Court of Appeal Criminal Division (London: Heinemann, 1970), p. 15.

37. Gwynn Nettler has asserted: "The governor of crime, as well as its generator, is culture. Every 'factor' that is selected for attention is possibly criminogenic, is embedded in a culture and reflects that culture. Every current explanation of crime looks at some facet of culture as central" (Nettler, Explaining Crime [New York: McGraw-Hill, 1974], p. 251).

38. New York State Special Commission on Attica, Attica (New York: Bantam Books, 1972), p. 93.

5

**PROSECUTORIAL
DISCRETION AND
SENTENCING—
A CASE STUDY**

Sentencing-related research in the past has generally been based on the assumption that sentencing decisions emanate from judges. In recent years, however, this assumption has been increasingly questioned, and attention has been drawn to the extremely powerful, and yet substantially hidden, role of the prosecutor. In the words of the director of research of the Vera Institute of Justice: "The recent felony disposition study in New York City . . . indicated that approximately 85% of all sentences were effectively decided before the judge got the case. This strongly suggests that the prosecutors have become the principal decision-makers in sentencing."[1]

The U.S. criminal justice system in some respects prides itself on openness and aspires to adhere to the stipulation in Article XIV of the U.S. Constitution: that no state shall "deprive any person of life, liberty, or property, without due process of law; nor deny to any person within its jurisdiction the equal protection of the laws."[2]

Yet the actual performance of the system is riddled with secrecy and inequity, particularly with respect to the plea bargaining process and the mode of operation of prosecutors within that process. It has been testified, for example:

> . . . the present plea bargaining system is
> arranged for the convenience of society, and
> . . . it falls most harshly on the poor and
> minorities. It should be perfectly obvious
> that when you keep most poor defendants in
> prison for three to six months before trial
> without any determination of guilt or

> innocence, the common law presumption of
> "innocent until proven guilty" becomes a mock-
> ery, and [the] resulting sentence plea becomes
> coercive of its very nature.[3]

The primary emphasis here is on prosecutorial discretion and concomitant sentencing, rather than on plea negotiation, which has already attracted a rather extensive literature.[4] "Discretion" is defined in the Random House Dictionary as "the power or right to decide or act according to one's own judgment." What is so remarkable about the discretion of prosecutors is that it is "almost total-- well nigh unreviewable in theory and even less reviewed in practice."[5] What is so unfortunate about this discretion is that in our experience, prosecutors vigorously resist attempts to open the discretion to public scrutiny--quite apart from the issue of curbing the discretion. *

Equally disturbing are the minimal qualifications needed for election. In 75 of Oklahoma's 77 counties, for example, a person need only have been a licensed attorney for two years, in addition to having resided in the state for two years, and in the district attorney district for three months, and having reached 25 years of age.[6] The electoral process, combined with the common practice of appointment of assistants of the same political affiliation, politicizes the office unduly and essentially invites its use for political aggrandizement. There is a strong incentive for the prosecutor to play to the gallery in order to build a political image, and quasi-judicial value judgments involving balance between deterrence and rehabilitation in the penalty structure, for example, may be shortchanged. Herein lies one of the sources of potentially profound variations in the actions of prosecutors from county to county. The ramifications in terms of such spatial variation are obvious. Prosecutorial discretion not only provides scope for the exercise of political influences through pressures from influential patrons, but also enables the purely personal preferences of prosecutors to act unrestrained in the criminal justice system. The late prosecutor for Oklahoma

----

*As a member of the Oklahoma Governor's Advisory Committee on Criminal Justice Standards and Goals, coauthor Harries advocated the goal of publication of sentencing rationales in felony convictions, in order to promote, indirectly, the reduction of sentence disparity. A motion to this effect was approved narrowly over strong opposition from law enforcement and prosecution representatives who apparently saw it as a curb on their powers.

County, Oklahoma, for example, had a strong personal penchant for pursuit of vendors of pornography; as a result, substantial criminal justice resources were allocated periodically to the prosecution of bookstore owners, theater owners, and such celebrities as Miss Nude Universe. That such emphasis was not uniformly applied throughout the state indicates one facet of the potential geographic impact of prosecutorial discretion. The importance of this geographic variation has apparently been recognized, at least in part, by the Institute for Law and Social Research--one of the publications in its important Prosecutor's Management Information System (PROMIS) Project will address "geographic and demographic patterns of crime" and will include examination of "possible differential processing by the criminal justice system of defendants from different areas. . . ."[7]

The following brief analysis of crimes of violence in Oklahoma and Tulsa Counties, Oklahoma, attempts to show, in an admittedly imperfect and crude way, how some elements of court-docket data may be used to obtain indicators of prosecutorial discretion and its related sentencing outcomes, and to compare them on a geographic basis.

THE DATA SOURCE

The data upon which this analysis is based were drawn from the court dockets in the Oklahoma County and Tulsa County courthouses as part of a larger project relating to all of the state's 77 counties. Information was recorded for all felonies in which the accused appeared in court.[8] The personal characteristics of the defendant, such as age, race, or sex, were not recorded, simply because they are not part of the docket. The emphasis was, rather, on significant procedural information, such as crimes for which the accused were charged, crimes for which defendants were sentenced, and details of the mode and characteristics of sentencing. (For further discussion, see p. 105.) It should be noted that all subsequent statistics reported here are based on the complete population, or whole subsets of the population, and significance levels that appear are provided for information rather than as inferential tools.

The Research Approach

The research paradigm adopted here rests primarily on a comparative accounting of violent crime events as they move through the criminal justice system from initial reporting to ultimate conviction or acquittal of defendants. One may imagine a pyramid, with numerous reported crimes constituting the base, tapering toward relatively few convictions at the apex. Within this accounting context, a number of related comparative issues may be approached. In relation to each issue, one may ask whether there are significant differences in the observed parameters for the two counties. If such differences are revealed, they may be regarded as surrogates for intercounty variations in individual and institutionalized behavior in the criminal justice system.

The discussion focuses on two problems:

Attrition, as measured by the difference between the number of crimes reported and the number for which offenders were sentenced;

Prosecutorial discretion (measured by dismissals, acquittals, and reductions in charges in the course of the criminal proceedings), and the associated pattern of sentencing, analyzed on three bases: intercounty variations in sentence weights, computed on the basis of the seriousness and magnitude of the punishment; sentence weight variations relating to mode of trial, and sentence weight variations relating to mode of appointment of defense counsel.

For the sake of both brevity and interest, the analysis was confined to crimes that are the equivalent of the FBI's Part I, or Index crimes of violence--those that are regarded as most serious and most frequent. Crime codes representing crimes defined by the Oklahoma statutes were reconciled as closely as possible with the FBI's violent index crime categories and abstracted from the larger file of docket data, which also contained information relating to other felony categories.

Attrition

As shown in Table 5.1, some 2,185 crimes of violence included in the FBI categories were reported in Oklahoma County in 1974, and 1,916 in Tulsa County. It is not suggested that these are true figures; they are used here merely as points of reference. In the same year (which is an imperfect match, because of delays in prosecution, earlier pending cases, and so forth), a total of 1,196 cases were prosecuted in the two county (district) courts, involving violent crimes comparable to the four FBI categories shown in Table 5.1. This represents 29.16 percent of the reported violent crimes; a complete breakdown in the format of a chi-square analysis is shown in Table 5.2. The largest contributions to the value of chi-square come from intercounty discrepancies in the assault and robbery categories. Of the 1,196 cases prosecuted, 642 (53.68 percent) resulted in sentencing (see Table 5.3).

TABLE 5.1

Reported Violent Crimes, by County, as a Proportion of Standard Metropolitan Statistical Area (SMSA) Totals

| Number of Crimes | Violent-Crime Category | | | | |
	Murder	Rape	Robbery	Aggravated Assault	Total
Oklahoma County	60	233	1,017	875	2,185
Oklahoma City SMSA[a,c]	74	269	1,117	1,217	2,677
Oklahoma County as percent of SMSA	81.1	86.6	91.0	71.9	81.6
Tulsa County	34	158	493	1,231	1,916
Tulsa SMSA[b,c]	40	173	531	1,327	2,071
Tulsa County as percent of SMSA	85.0	91.3	92.8	92.8	92.5

[a]Canadian, Cleveland, McClain, Oklahoma, and Pottowatomie Counties.
[b]Creek, Mayes, Osage, Rogers, Tulsa, and Wagoner Counties.
[c]Actual, rather than estimated, totals.
Sources: Oklahoma State Bureau of Investigation, 1974 Annual Report: Crime in Oklahoma (Oklahoma City: OSBI, 1975), Part 4, pp. 60, 63; Federal Bureau of Investigation, Crime in the United States, 1974 (Washington, D.C.: U.S. Government Printing Office, 1975), Table 5, pp. 84, 89.

If crimes reported to the police are used as a base, Oklahoma County prosecuted and sentenced in a higher proportion of cases than did Tulsa County, and dismissed and acquitted in lower proportions. Similar observations are valid if prosecutions are used as the base-- among cases prosecuted, Oklahoma County sentenced over 12 percent more than did Tulsa for similar crimes of violence. Though the assertion of the Oklahoma County District Attorney that his office had an "eighty-five to ninety-five per cent" rate of conviction would appear questionable (at least for violent crimes), an operating hypothesis to the effect that Oklahoma County is "tougher" than Tulsa would appear to be justified.[9] The firing of an assistant district attorney who was supposedly responsible for dismissing excessive numbers of cases at preliminary hearings also tends to substantiate the hard line in Oklahoma County,[10] as did the eulogy for the district attorney (Curtis Harris) following his death on May 27, 1976; he was referred to as a "tough law and order man."

TABLE 5.2

Cases Prosecuted, by County

| Crime Involved | County | | Total |
	Oklahoma	Tulsa	
Murder	70.00[a]	38.00	108.00
	60.05[b]	47.95	108.00
	1.65[c]	2.06	3.71
Rape	41.00	46.00	87.00
	48.37	38.63	87.00
	1.12	1.41	2.53
Robbery	295.00	184.00	479.00
	266.33	212.67	479.00
	3.09	3.86	6.95
Assault	259.00	263.00	522.00
	290.24	231.76	522.00
	3.36	4.21	7.57
Total	665.00	531.00	1,196.00
	665.00	531.00	1,196.00
	9.22	11.54	20.76

Note: Chi-square = 20.77 with 3 df's (degrees of freedom) and p (probability) = 0.0002.
[a]Observed.
[b]Expected.
[c]Cell chi-square.
Source: Authors' computations, based on field data.

Analysis of dismissals and acquittals provides a basis for more detailed comparisons between the two counties. Dismissals were most numerous, and Table 5.4 reconciles them with the FBI crime categories and the counties. Tulsa County dismissed proportionately more rape and assault cases than did Oklahoma, but fewer in the murder and robbery categories. Although intercounty differences were not exceptional in any given crime category, the fact remains that in cumulative terms Tulsa County dismissed 14.18 percent more of its cases (Table 5.3). Acquittals occur at about the same relative frequency in both counties (accounting for few cases), and will not be discussed further.

TABLE 5.3

Comparative Dispositions of Reported Violent Crimes

Status Category of Case	Oklahoma County			Tulsa County			Total Frequency
	Total Cases	Percent of Reported Cases	Percent of Prosecuted Cases	Total Cases	Percent of Reported Cases	Percent of Prosecuted Cases	
Reported	2,185	--	--	1,916	--	--	4,101
Prosecuted[a]	665	30.43	--	531	27.71	--	1,196
Dismissed	195	8.92	29.32	231	12.06	43.50	426
Acquitted	25	1.14	3.76	24	1.25	4.52	49
Sentenced[b]	393	17.99	59.10	249	13.00	46.89	642
Other[c]	52	2.38	7.82	27	1.41	5.08	79

[a]In which the accused appeared in court; excludes attempts.
[b]Includes deferred judgments, which are technically not sentences.
[c]Pending and awaiting sentence.

Sources: Authors' computations, based on field data; Oklahoma State Bureau of Investigation, 1974 Annual Report: Crime in Oklahoma (Oklahoma City: OSBI, 1975), Part 4, pp. 60, 63.

TABLE 5.4

Percent of Cases Dismissed in Each County,
by Crime Category

	County	
Crime Category	Oklahoma	Tulsa
Murder	4.17	2.62
Rape	6.25	9.17
Robbery	37.50	31.88
Aggravated assault	52.08	56.33
Total	100.00	100.00

Source: Authors' computations, based on field data.

In aggregate terms, attrition through dismissals and acquittals accounted for 33.08 of the prosecutions in Oklahoma County, and 48.02 percent in Tulsa, again reinforcing the apparently tougher prosecutorial posture in Oklahoma County.

Prosecutorial Discretion

The influence of the district attorney in the judicial process is overwhelming, and may involve the initial decision to prosecute, a subsequent decision to dismiss, and the process of plea negotiation, which is often linked to the ultimate act of sentencing. Many judges, in fact, will freely admit that they give relatively little consideration to sentencing and often prefer to rely on the recommendation of the prosecutor.

Since the gravity of a crime for which a defendant is originally charged is rarely increased,[11] one measure of prosecutorial discretion lies in the difference, if any, between the original charge and the crime for which the individual may be subsequently sentenced. Table 5.5 shows the extent to which original charges were later modified, by counties. Tulsa County prosecutors clearly had a higher propensity to reduce charges as compared to those in Oklahoma County. One offence category, murder, may be selected to illustrate further the charge reduction process (see Table 5.6). In both counties, the majority of first- and second-degree murder charges were eventually reduced, or the cases had not been disposed of at the time the data were recorded. In most identifiable cases, murder charges tended to become manslaughter in the course of the

TABLE 5.5

Modifications of Original Charges, by County

Original Charge	Oklahoma County		Tulsa County	
	Total Cases	Percent Changed	Total Cases	Percent Changed
Murder	70	31.43	38	44.74
Rape	41	19.51	46	21.74
Robbery	295	7.12	184	11.96
Assault	259	16.99	263	24.71
Total	665	75.05	531	103.15

Source: Authors' computations, based on field data.

TABLE 5.6

Modifications of Murder Charges, by County

	Original Charge			
	Oklahoma County		Tulsa County	
Subsequent Charge	First-Degree Murder	Second-Degree Murder	First-Degree Murder	Second-Degree Murder
Not sentenced*	6	12	2	9
First-degree murder	5	1	1	0
Second-degree murder	2	16	0	3
First-degree manslaughter	1	14	2	10
Second-degree manslaughter	0	4	0	2
Accessory	0	0	0	1
Total	14	47	5	25

*At date of field observation; includes dismissals, cases pending, and so on.

Source: Authors' computations, based on field data.

judicial process, with the practical result that potential punishment was reduced from life imprisonment to a term of one to four years. Similarly, a charge of assault with intent to kill tended to become aggravated assault or assault with a deadly weapon or simple assault in those cases in which charge reduction occurred.

How does the pattern of sentencing compare between the metropolitan areas--what is the ultimate product of prosecutorial discretion? An offender in Oklahoma may be sentenced as the result of a plea of guilty, a jury trial, or a judge trial. Procedural considerations suggest that severity of sentence will be related to mode of judgment. It is in the interest of the judicial system, with its limited resources, to minimize the number of jury or judge trials. Of the offenders sentenced in Tulsa and Oklahoma Counties in 1974, some 85 percent pled guilty, suggesting the effectiveness of the plea negotiation process as an expeditor of case disposition. It is to be expected that a negotiated plea will contain an element of sentence amelioration or charge modification (or both), in return for which the guilty plea is entered. A trial, on the other hand, which is expensive and time consuming for the state, will usually result in "rather less generous treatment than [that for the defendant] who has negotiated."[12] Jury trials in Oklahoma are complicated by the fact that jury sentencing may occur in noncapital cases. In the present study, 14 percent of the cases involving sentencing had jury trials, and less than 1 percent judge trials.

Several sentencing options are open in the event that the accused pleads guilty or is found guilty by trial. Sentences of death, imprisonment, jail, fine, and probation are all possibilities--some in combination, such as fine and imprisonment. Other options that may be statutorily permissible are deferred and suspended sentences. The sentence deferment procedure is described in an Oklahoma statute as follows:

> Upon a verdict or plea of guilty, but before a
> judgment of guilty, the court may, without enter-
> ing a judgment of guilt and with the consent of the
> defendant, defer further proceedings and place the
> defendant on probation under the supervision of the
> State Department of Corrections upon the condi-
> tions of probation prescribed by court. Such con-
> ditions may include restitution when applicable.
> Upon completion of the probation term, which pro-
> bation term under this procedure shall not exceed
> two years, the defendant shall be discharged with-
> out a court judgment of guilt, and the verdict or
> plea of guilty shall be expunged from the record

> and said charge shall be dismissed with prejudice
> to any further action. Upon violation of the condi-
> tions of the probation, the court may enter a judg-
> ment of guilt and proceed as provided. . . . The
> deferred judgment procedure described in this
> section shall only apply to defendants not having
> been previously convicted of a felony.[13]

While a deferred judgment is not technically a sentence at all,
a suspended sentence involves the release of the individual, but not
until after the actual pronouncement of sentence:

> Whenever any person shall be convicted in any
> court of record for any crime other than murder,
> manslaughter or arson, the Judge trying said
> cause [sic] may, after sentence, suspend said
> judgment and sentence, and allow said person so
> convicted to be released upon his own recogni-
> zance.[14]

In the event that the individual released in the manner described above

> . . . has been guilty of a violation of any law
> after his said release, or is habitually associat-
> ing with lewd or vicious persons, or is indulging
> in vicious habits, in that event said Court shall
> cause a warrant to be issued for said person,
> and he shall be delivered forthwith to the place
> of confinement to which originally sentenced, and
> shall serve out the full term for which he had
> originally been sentenced.[15]

Deferred and suspended sentences, then, may be regarded, in
the words of the statute, as "mild and ambulatory." Accordingly,
in the process of developing a sentence weighting scheme to enable
the generalized quantification of sentences, deferred and suspended
sentences were both allocated the lowest weight. Other sentences
were assigned weights based on the severity and magnitude of the
punishment. Thus probation was assigned the lowest weight, and
imprisonment the highest. Death sentences were disregarded since
the death penalty is currently moribund. A total weight was calculated for each sentence, based on the sum of weights for each
mode of punishment. Punishment weights were computed on the
basis of the mode weight multiplied by the quartile value. Table 5.7
shows the weights employed.[16]

TABLE 5.7

Sentence Weights

Sentence	Mode Weight	Maximum Possible
Deferred	0.25	0.25
Suspended	0.25	0.25
Probation	0.25	1.00
Fine	1.00	4.00
Jail	2.00	8.00
Prison	4.00	16.00

Source: Compiled by the authors.

A couple of examples may serve to illustrate the determina-
tion of weights. Case number 3237 in Oklahoma County was a first-
degree rape. The sentence was imprisonment, with the number of
years (10) falling in the third quartile. This was multiplied by the
mode weight (4) to provide an imprisonment weight of 12. However,
the sentence was suspended, overriding the imprisonment, and
forcing the total weight down to 0.25. Case number 3045 in Tulsa
County, a first-degree manslaughter, received eight years' probation, falling in the fourth (highest) quartile (weight = 1.00), plus
two years' imprisonment (first quartile, weight = 4.00) for a total
weight of 5.00. In practice, the weights in each county ranged from
0.25 to 16.00, with an overall mean of 6.41 for N = 642.

In Oklahoma County, the mean sentence weight in cases excluding suspended sentences or deferred judgments was 10.45; in
Tulsa County, 6.66. These weights included multiple punishments
such as imprisonment and probation. A more detailed view of intercounty sentence patterns is presented in Table 5.8, in which mean
sentence weights for particular crime categories are compared. In
three of the five categories, Oklahoma County exhibited a higher
weight than did Tulsa. Broken down at this level of detail, however,
parameters become somewhat ambiguous, since the element of plea
negotiation is essentially lost. Thus a relatively serious felony may
be reduced to a felony of lower degree, or to a misdemeanor, for
which the sentence may be relatively heavy. Such sentence reduction is further complicated by apparently consistently different patterns in sentencing, by county, and possibly by category of crime
within counties. In Oklahoma County, for example, probation was
used as a form of punishment only four times in connection with the

393 cases under review, and three of those decisions emanated from the same judge. In Tulsa County, probation was used much more frequently and was distributed more randomly among judges. The virtual absence of probation in Oklahoma County probably influences sentence weights in the direction of severity.

TABLE 5.8

Mean Sentence Weights for Selected Crimes, by County

Crime Category	Oklahoma County		Tulsa County	
	Mean Weight	N	Mean Weight	N
Assault with a deadly weapon	1.56	35	4.17	26
Armed robbery	12.12	124	9.42	59
Assault with intent to kill	5.13	28	4.94	17
Manslaughter (first degree)	5.06	21	9.16	14
Rape (first degree)	9.73	12	5.95	5

Note: "Selected crimes" here means crimes for which defendants are sentenced, which may differ categorically from crimes with which individuals are charged. The crimes shown here only partially represent the four types shown, for example, in Table 5.1.
Source: Authors' computations, based on field data.

A more generalized perspective on intercounty sentencing variations may be obtained by examining weights converted to quartile values in a chi-square model (see Table 5.9). The largest row contribution to the value of chi-square was provided by the highest-weight quartile, in which Oklahoma County was substantially underpredicted and Tulsa County overpredicted. In the lowest quartile, the reverse is true, but the contribution to chi-square was minimal. In the second and third quartiles, Oklahoma County was overpredicted, Tulsa County underpredicted. Study of the frequency distributions indicates that Tulsa County's is flat, while Oklahoma County's is quite polarized, with about 39 percent in the fourth quartile and 34 percent in the first. The virtual absence of probation in the latter county may reduce statistical smoothing and account for the bimodal character of the weights.

TABLE 5.9

Sentence Weights Compared by Quartiles, by County

Quartile Value of Weights	County		Total
	Oklahoma	Tulsa	
1 (lowest)	135.00[a]	73.00	208.00
	127.33[b]	80.67	208.00
	0.46[c]	0.73	1.19
2	51.00	59.00	110.00
	67.34	42.66	110.00
	3.96	6.26	10.22
3	54.00	64.00	118.00
	72.23	45.77	118.00
	4.60	7.26	11.86
4 (highest)	153.00	53.00	206.00
	126.10	79.90	206.00
	5.74	9.05	14.79
Total	393.00	249.00	642.00
	393.00	249.00	642.00
	14.76	23.30	38.07

[a]Observed.
[b]Predicted.
[c]Cell chi-square.

Note: Total chi-square = 38.07 with 3 df's and p > chi-square = 0.0001.

Source: Authors' computations, based on field data.

As suggested earlier, it is to be expected that the manner in which a verdict is reached will be related to severity of sentencing, with a dichotomy between leniency for guilty pleas and harshness for judge or jury trials. Table 5.10 shows mean sentence weights for guilty pleas and trials, by county. If mean weights for judge trials are disregarded owing to their small frequency (N = 5), the expectation is validated, and interest turns to the question of inter-county variation. In both counties, jury-trial weights were almost identical, on the order of two to three times as severe as weights derived from guilty pleas. The latter, which, based on large N's, differ substantially between the counties, with the direction of the difference again supporting the apparent hard line in Oklahoma County.

TABLE 5.10

Mean Sentence Weights for Guilty Pleas and Trials, by County

Oklahoma County			Tulsa County		
Guilty Plea (N = 329)	Jury Trial (N = 62)	Judge Trial (N = 2)	Guilty Plea (N = 218)	Jury Trial (N = 28)	Judge Trial (N = 3)
6.24	11.63	1.13	4.52	11.42	10.75

Source: Authors' computations, based on field data.

Just as the manner in which a guilty verdict is reached has an impact on sentence severity, so the manner in which defense coun- sel is appointed may be hypothesized to be related to the sentencing outcome.[17] It is suggested that court-appointed counsel may be less effective defenders as compared to attorneys retained privately by the accused. However, some district attorneys maintain that, in fact, public defenders know the criminal law very well, and that the relatively severe sentences associated with their cases are the product of relatively serious offenses committed by their clients rather than of counsel's level of competence or motivation. Table 5.11 shows mean sentence weights for appointed and retained coun- sel, by county. If sentence weights are analyzed as quartile values with respect to mode of attorney appointment, then in Oklahoma County 26.02 percent of the sentenced cases fell in the lowest quar- tile and involved privately retained counsel. More than 27 percent were in the severest quartile and involved court-appointed defenders. Comparable values for Tulsa County are 24.29 percent and 15.79 percent (see Table 5.12).

TABLE 5.11

Mean Sentence Weights for Court-Appointed and Privately Retained Counsel, by County

Oklahoma County		Tulsa County	
Court Appointed	Privately Retained	Court Appointed	Privately Retained
9.86	4.61	7.88	3.57

Source: Authors' computations, based on field data.

TABLE 5.12

Percent Distribution of Sentence Weights by Mode of
Attorney Appointment, by County

Sentence Weight Quartile	Oklahoma County (N = 392)[a]		Tulsa County (N = 247)[b]	
	Percent of Cases by Mode of Appointment		Percent of Cases by Mode of Appointment	
	Court Appointed	Privately Retained	Court Appointed	Privately Retained
1 (lowest)	8.42	26.02	5.26	24.29
2	3.57	9.18	7.29	16.19
3	7.91	5.87	12.96	12.96
4 (highest)	27.04	11.99	15.79	5.26
Total	100.00		100.00	

[a]One missing value, implying self-defense.
[b]Two missing values, implying self-defense.
Source: Authors' computations, based on field data.

Intracounty and intercounty differences in weights are both
notable, and can only rekindle questions relating to the effectiveness of counsel appointed publicly or retained privately and, yet
again, to the relative leniency of Tulsa County.

CONCLUSION

Analysis of docket data descriptive of case attrition, prosecutorial discretion, and sentencing in Oklahoma and Tulsa Counties
suggests, with respect to violent crimes, that an offender in Oklahoma County is more likely to be prosecuted, less likely to have his
case dismissed or be acquitted (and thus more likely to be sentenced), and more likely to draw a severe punishment if sentenced,
as compared to Tulsa County. Thus, the tough prosecutorial stance
projected by the Oklahoma County District Attorney's office appears
to produce the sanctions deemed desirable by that office, though the
long-term, or even short-term, impact on criminality in Oklahoma
County is not measurable. While the intercounty differences in sentencing and other procedures may reflect real cultural variations,
it is at least equally probable that causes may be traced to the

attitudes and actions of a few powerful individuals in the criminal
justice system.

TABLE 5.13

Population-Specific Rates of Reported Violent Crimes, 1974

| Crime Category | County | |
	Oklahoma	Tulsa
Murder	11.39	8.46
Rape	44.21	39.30
Robbery	192.98	122.64
Aggravated assault	166.03	306.22

Note: Rate per 100,000 inhabitants, based on 1970 census data.
Sources: Oklahoma State Bureau of Investigation, 1974 Annual
Report: Crime in Oklahoma (Oklahoma City: OSBI, 1975), Table 1,
and field data. Computations by authors.

The ultimate question is whether the hard line in Oklahoma
County has an effect on the crime rate. Since questions of this type
involve evaluation of what is essentially an uncontrolled experiment,
no scientifically acceptable answer is obtainable, and the public is
generally left to draw its own conclusions from rhetorical asser-
tions emanating from various criminal justice officials. As no
crime victimization surveys have been conducted in either county,
the only available evidence consists of the notoriously unreliable reported crime statistics ultimately incorporated in the Uniform
Crime Reports of the FBI (see Table 5.13). Time series analysis
comparing the Oklahoma City and Tulsa Standard Metropolitan
Statistical Areas (SMSAs) suggests that in the period 1968-75, all
FBI index crime rates rose more steeply in the former area. However, no causal inferences can be made--one can merely observe
that in the murder, rape, and robbery categories, Tulsa County had
lower reported rates and rates of increase than did Oklahoma County.
Inexplicably, the rate of assault in Tulsa County was almost twice
as high as in Oklahoma County.[18] Even if definitional ambiguities
are considered, a difference of the order of magnitude shown still
defies explanation, except as a large-scale systematic reporting
error in either or both counties. Since no plausible connection between crime rates and prosecution and sentencing practices can be

established, one must return to the mundane conclusion that accused persons are, in several respects, treated quite differently in the counties under review--a violation of the principle of equality under the law. Current legislative initiative in Oklahoma seeking to create mandatory minimum preparole sentences fails to approach problems of sentence disparity and extremes in sentencing, as a significant recent report has noted.[19] It is indeed unfortunate that important alternatives such as presumptive sentencing have not, to date, been given serious consideration in Oklahoma or in many other states. It is equally disturbing that the procedural secrecy and apparent inconsistency in the treatment of defendants between jurisdictions-- traceable in considerable measure to the personal preferences of prosecutors--continue to thrive unscathed in spite of an environment that seems to be increasingly disposed toward reform.[20]

NOTES

1. Lucy Friedman, quoted in John C. Ruhnka, Research Priorities in Sentencing (Denver: National Center for State Courts, 1975), pp. 38-39.

2. U.S. Constitution, Article XIV, Sec. 1.

3. Judge Thomas R. Jones, New York Supreme Court, Second Judicial District, quoted in Ruhnka, op. cit., p. 11.

4. It is acknowledged that plea negotiation may occur in conjunction with judges and probation agencies, as well as with prosecutors; however, the most important role is that of the prosecutor. See John Barbara, June Morrison, and Horace Cunningham, "Plea Bargaining--Bargain Justice?" Criminology 14 (May 1976): 56.

5. Jack M. Kress, "Progress and Prosecution," Annals, American Academy of Political and Social Science 423 (January 1976): 109.

6. Oklahoma Statutes Annotated, 19, Sec. 215.2 (1976 Supplement). In the two largest metropolitan counties, Tulsa and Oklahoma, which are the subject of the subsequent analysis, the minimum age is 28, and five years of law practice are needed.

7. Institute for Law and Social Research, Geographic and Demographic Patterns of Crime (Washington, D.C.: Institute for Law and Social Research, forthcoming).

8. "A felony is a crime which is, or may be, punishable with death, or by imprisonment in the State prison" Oklahoma Statutes Annotated, 21, Sec. 5 (1975).

9. "A Close Look at the Court of Criminal Appeals," Daily Oklahoman, January 13, 1974, pp. 21, 23.

10. "Lawyer Outlines Job Sore Points," Daily Oklahoman, January 10, 1974, p. 39.

11. "If it appear by the testimony that the facts proved constitute an offense of a higher nature than that charged in the indictment or information, the court may direct the jury to be discharged, and all proceedings on the indictment or information to be suspended . . ." (Oklahoma Statutes Annotated, 22, Sec. 841 [1975]).

12. A. S. Blumberg, Criminal Justice (Chicago: Quadrangle Books, 1970), pp. 28-31.

13. Oklahoma Statutes Annotated, 22, Sec. 991c (1975).

14. Oklahoma Statutes Annotated, 22, Sec. 991 (1975).

15. Oklahoma Statutes Annotated, 22, Sec. 992 (1975).

16. This scheme is similar in principle to that employed by the federal court system for the comparative analysis of sentences. See Administrative Office of the U.S. Courts, Federal Offenders in the U.S. District Courts--1969 (Washington, D.C.: U.S. Government Printing Office, 1971), Table 10, p. 52, and Chapter 6 of this study.

17. See U.S. Congress, Senate, Committee on the Judiciary, Hearing Before the Subcommittee on Criminal Laws and Procedures, 92d Cong., 2d sess., cited in Reform of the Federal Criminal Laws (Washington, D.C.: U.S. Government Printing Office, 1972), p. 3907; in an analysis of federal court data, it was found that "the average prison percentages nationwide for defendants in the appointed counsel subset were consistently higher than the percentages for defendants in the private counsel subset."

18. A representative of the Records Division of the Tulsa Police Department suggested that the discrepancy is probably due to differences in reporting practices, rather than to intercounty behavioral variations. The dividing line between simple assault and aggravated assault is rather subjective. "Felonious (aggravated) assault" may involve firearms, knives or cutting instruments, and other dangerous weapons, including "hands, fists, feet, etc." To be regarded as felonious, "the attack must result in serious personal injury." "Serious" is not defined (Oklahoma State Bureau of Investigation, Oklahoma Uniform Crime Reporting Guide [Oklahoma City: OSBI, 1973], Part 4, pp. 19-23).

19. The Twentieth Century Fund Task Force on Criminal Sentencing, Fair and Certain Punishment (New York: McGraw-Hill, 1976), p. 17.

20. By way of postscript, it may be pointed out that a separate study conducted by the Oklahoma Crime Commission has drawn attention to differences in the criminal justice process between Oklahoma and Tulsa Counties. The findings of that analysis

confirm suppositions made here, including that regarding the relative severity of Oklahoma County, which reduces fewer defendants
to misdemeanant status and incarcerates more (Oklahoma Crime
Commission, 1977 Oklahoma Criminal Justice Comprehensive Action Plan [Oklahoma City: Oklahoma Crime Commission, 1976], p.
128).

6

**SENTENCING
VARIATION:
EMPIRICAL
EXAMPLES**

In this chapter, several studies of geographical variations in sentencing are summarized. The first, and most general, examines sentence severity in the federal court system and develops a tentative model designed to account for statistical variation in the patterns that are illustrated. The second study focuses on the state of Oklahoma, and looks specifically at regional patterns in felony drug sentencing. In the latter study, it is suggested that the cultural history of an area may strongly influence sentencing behavior and lead to significant intraregional disparities. Finally, other selected sentencing studies are discussed.

SENTENCING IN U.S. JUDICIAL DISTRICTS

In recent years, considerable attention has been paid to sentence disparities in the federal courts.[1] The light sentence (three years' probation and a $10,000 fine) imposed on former Vice President Agnew following tax evasion charges focused concern on what has been termed the "anarchy" of federal sentencing.[2] Agnew's sentence was compared to several received by other individuals on or about the same day that he was sentenced; for example, a Sacramento draftsman had been sentenced, in municipal court, to 70 days in prison for fishing offenses; in federal court in El Paso, six Mexicans had received 100 days for illegal entry into the United States.[3] More recently, a special issue of <u>Judicature</u> has dealt with sentencing, and the television networks have devoted a good deal of time to the topic.[4] At the time of this writing, there is considerable pressure to standardize sentencing in the federal courts. To illustrate the current situation, however, we draw on an earlier study (cited in Note 1 of this chapter).

The study has two major objectives. First, it examines the idea that some aspects of sentencing in federal courts may reveal significant variations in their regional distributions. More formally, this is the examination of the hypothesis that variations in sentencing are randomly distributed, quantitatively and qualitatively, around the judicial districts. Second, the study reports on a model developed to explain, in a statistical sense, observed variations in sentencing patterns.

Graphic Analysis of Imprisonment and Probation

Two general sentences--imprisonment and probation--constitute a large majority of all sentences. Other alternatives available to the courts, including fines, deportation, suspended sentences and remitted fines (and combinations of these), are not considered in this section.

In 1970, 36,356 cases involving criminal defendants were disposed of in U.S. courts; of these, 78 percent of the defendants were convicted. Of those convicted, 39 percent were imprisoned, 45 percent placed on probation, and 15 percent given fines or other sentences.[5] If special-offense categories (immigration laws, wagering-tax laws, and federal regulatory statutes) are excluded, the proportion of defendants imprisoned rises to 44 percent, the use of probation increases to 53 percent, while only 3 percent receive fines or other sentences. When we consider average and relative sentence weights, all offense classes are included. However, data on the use of probation are not available for the special offenses and they are consequently excluded when we consider probation measures.

Four types of measurement will be used here: average sentence weight, relative sentence weight, percent of defendants placed on probation, and relative use of probation. In order to facilitate the comparison of sentence severity by district, the Administrative Office of the U.S. Courts developed a sentence weighting system in 1964 known as the average sentence weight. The weights range from 0 for suspended sentences and probation without supervision, to 50 for prison sentences of over 120 months. In 1970, the average weight value per defendant was 5.9 overall, 2.5 for probationers under supervision, and 12.1 for persons imprisoned.[6]

Relative sentence weight measures the differences between the actual average sentence weight and the expected average sentence weight that would result if each conviction received a sentence equivalent to the national average for that offense class. For example, the 1970 average sentence weight for Maine was 2.8; the expected average sentence weight for the crimes committed in that

district was 4.7. The relative sentence weight was -40.4, reflect-
ing the percent difference between actual and expected average
sentence weights.[7]

The percentage placed on probation is adequately self-
explanatory.[8] Relative use of probation is analogous to relative
sentence weight, in that it compares the actual percent placed on
probation to a mathematical expectancy based on the national average use of probation for eight offense classes. Thus in Maryland in
1970, 57.1 percent of the 413 sentenced defendants were placed on
probation. The expected proportion, based on the offense structure
(but excluding detailed characteristics of defendants), was 52.4
percent. The relative use of probation is the actual percent of defendants placed on probation that are above or below the expected
value.

In Maryland, the difference between the actual and expected
values is 4.7 points, which is 9 percent higher than the expected
value; 9 percent is the relative-use-of-probation figure used in our
analysis. Negative values may also occur. Courts in West Virginia's North District actually placed 13.9 percent on probation (15
of 108 sentenced defendants), but a value of 48.9 percent was expected. The difference (35 percent) is 71.6 percent less than the
expected value. In this case the relative-use-of-probation data
value is -71.6 percent.[9]

It must be reemphasized that the study deals only with federal
offenses, and thus touches on only a small proportion of the court
cases in the United States. In addition there is no attempt here to
take into account the age of the offender, prior criminal record, or
recommendations of various auxiliary court agencies. There is a
simplifying assumption that such factors will be randomly distributed
throughout the districts, and will be substantially equalized through
the use of district totals.

Map 6.1 is an outline of federal judicial districts (the Louisiana
Middle District, created in 1971, is excluded here but does appear
on the maps in Chapter 7). Table 6.1 lists corresponding district
names.

Map 6.2 illustrates the distribution of average sentence
weights among districts. These ranged from a low of 2.6 in Louisiana West to a high of 12.7 in Alabama South. The map shading is
based on a quartile division of districts; the districts were rank
ordered by average sentence weights, then divided into four groups
of equal frequency. In Map 6.2, as in Map 6.4, each quartile is
shaded with increasing intensity from light (termed most favorable
to defendants) to dark (least favorable to defendants).

In Map 6.2, a number of district regions are prominent.
Northeastern districts, Texas South, Louisiana, and districts from

MAP 6.1: Federal Judicial Districts

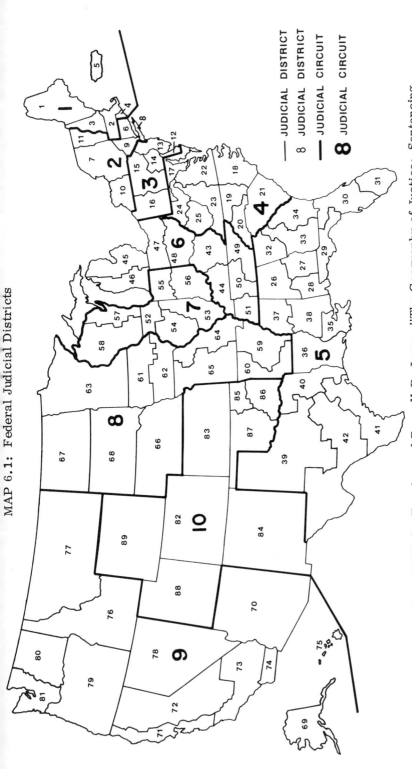

Source: Adapted from Keith D. Harries and Russell P. Lura, "The Geography of Justice: Sentencing Variations in U.S. Judicial Districts," Judicature 57, no. 9 (1974): 392–401. Data source was: Administrative Office of the U.S. Courts, Federal Offenders in the United States District Courts--1970 (Washington, D.C.: U.S. Government Printing Office, 1972), p. 60.

TABLE 6.1

Key to U.S. Court Circuits and Districts Shown in Map 6.1

First Circuit
1. Maine
2. Massachusetts
3. New Hampshire
4. Rhode Island
5. Puerto Rico

Second Circuit
6. Connecticut
7. New York North
8. New York East
9. New York South
10. New York West
11. Vermont

Third Circuit
12. Delaware
13. New Jersey
14. Pennsylvania East
15. Pennsylvania Middle
16. Pennsylvania West

Fourth Circuit
17. Maryland
18. North Carolina East
19. North Carolina Middle
20. North Carolina West

21. South Carolina
22. Virginia East
23. Virginia West
24. West Virginia North
25. West Virginia South

Fifth Circuit
26. Alabama North
27. Alabama Middle
28. Alabama South
29. Florida North
30. Florida Middle
31. Florida South
32. Georgia North
33. Georgia Middle
34. Georgia South
35. Louisiana East
36. Louisiana West
37. Mississippi North
38. Mississippi South
39. Texas North
40. Texas East
41. Texas South
42. Texas West

Sixth Circuit
43. Kentucky East

44. Kentucky West
45. Michigan East
46. Michigan West
47. Ohio North
48. Ohio South
49. Tennessee East
50. Tennessee Middle
51. Tennessee West

Seventh Circuit
52. Illinois North
53. Illinois East
54. Illinois South
55. Indiana North
56. Indiana South
57. Wisconsin East
58. Wisconsin West

Eighth Circuit
59. Arkansas East
60. Arkansas West
61. Iowa North
62. Iowa South
63. Minnesota
64. Missouri East
65. Missouri West
66. Nebraska

67. North Dakota
68. South Dakota

Ninth Circuit
69. Alaska
70. Arizona
71. California North
72. California East
73. California Central
74. California South
75. Hawaii
76. Idaho
77. Montana
78. Nevada
79. Oregon
80. Washington East
81. Washington West

Tenth Circuit
82. Colorado
83. Kansas
84. New Mexico
85. Oklahoma North
86. Oklahoma East
87. Oklahoma West
88. Utah
89. Wyoming

Source: Administrative Office of the U.S. Courts.

MAP 6.2: Average Sentence Weights

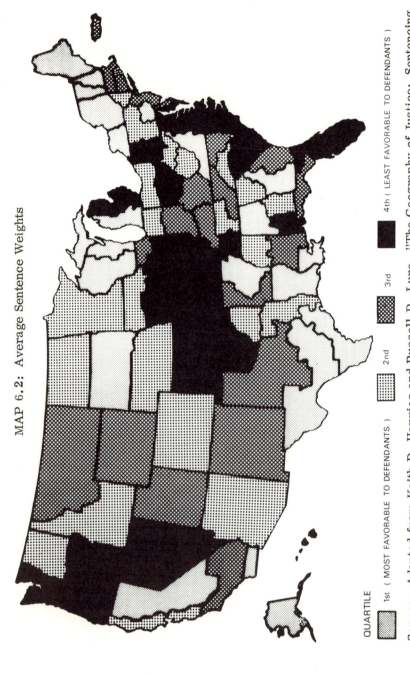

QUARTILE

1st (MOST FAVORABLE TO DEFENDANTS)

2nd

3rd

4th (LEAST FAVORABLE TO DEFENDANTS)

Source: Adapted from Keith D. Harries and Russell P. Lura, "The Geography of Justice: Sentencing Variations in U.S. Judicial Districts," Judicature 57, no. 9 (1974): 392–401. Data source was: Administrative Office of the U.S. Courts, Federal Offenders in the United States District Courts--1970 (Washington, D.C.: U.S. Government Printing Office, 1972), p. 60.

Arkansas East to Georgia Middle are lowest in average sentence weight. With the exception of Michigan East, a belt of low average-sentence-weight districts stretches from Maine to North and South Dakota. The western districts are fairly mixed; California ranges from low to moderately high, while Washington West, Oregon, and Nevada reveal very high weights. The West South Central districts also have a mixed pattern, ranging from very high in Oklahoma North and West to very low in Texas West and South.

A band of low average-sentence-weight districts separates the relatively high South Atlantic area from the largest contiguous group of high-weight districts--from Oklahoma North and West through Kansas, Missouri, Iowa South, and Illinois. The districts in this area are all in the fourth or highest quartile.

The core areas most unfavorable to defendants include this central region, plus the South Atlantic area, and districts from Washington West to Nevada. On the other hand, two areas, one stretching from Maine across the North Central part of the nation to the Dakotas, Nebraska, and across to Colorado, and the other extending from Texas West to North Carolina West, include districts most favorable to defendants.

Theoretically, the relative sentence weight should exhibit little spatial variation. If all federal judges treated similar cases similarly, and if legally relevant factors were indeed randomly distributed throughout the 89 districts, the resulting map would be devoid of variation. As Map 6.3 shows, this is not the case. The pattern resembles that of Map 6.2; average sentence weight and relative sentence weight are rather strongly correlated spatially.

The northern tier from Maine to the Dakotas retains its low rank, and California, and Texas South through Louisiana West and Arkansas East, are the two other main concentrations of districts that are apparently most favorable to defendants.

High relative sentence weights are found in a belt running from Washington West through Arizona and New Mexico, into Texas, Oklahoma, Missouri, Illinois, Kentucky, and on to the Atlantic Coast, with the exceptions of Virginia West and North Carolina West. There are two areas of very high relative sentence weight: Oklahoma West (with a relative weight of 44.9) northeastward to Illinois South (28.8), and Kentucky East and Tennessee East to the South Atlantic coast.

Three districts are prominent for their difference in rank between average and relative sentence weights. Texas West was in the first, or lowest, quartile in average sentence weight, and in the third quartile in relative sentence weight, indicating a more severe pattern of actual sentencing than the offense structure would be expected to indicate. Pennsylvania West is in the fourth (most severe) quartile in average sentence weight, but in the second quartile in

MAP 6.3: Relative Sentence Weights

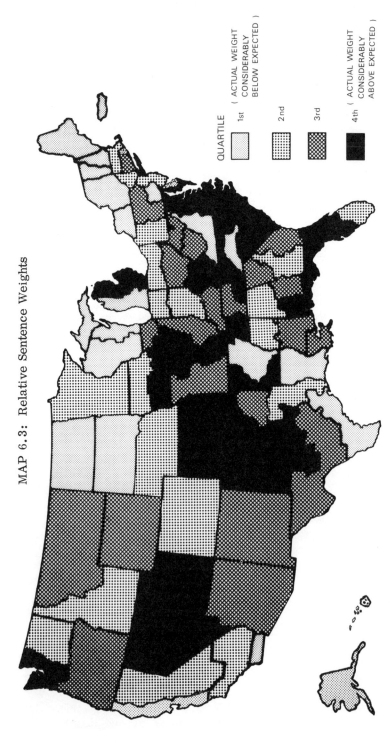

QUARTILE

1st (ACTUAL WEIGHT
CONSIDERABLY
BELOW EXPECTED)

2nd

3rd

4th (ACTUAL WEIGHT
CONSIDERABLY
ABOVE EXPECTED)

Source: Adapted from Keith D. Harries and Russell P. Lura, "The Geography of Justice: Sentencing Variations in U.S. Judicial Districts," Judicature 57, no. 9 (1974): 392–401. Data source was: Administrative Office of the U.S. Courts, Federal Offenders in the United States District Courts—1970 (Washington, D.C.: U.S. Government Printing Office, 1972), p. 60.

relative weight; Puerto Rico moves from the third quartile to the first, indicating, as does Pennsylvania West, less severe sentencing patterns than would be predicted on the basis of offense structure, in spite of high actual weights.

Study of the variability of average and relative sentence weights through the conversion of data values to standard deviation units draws attention to districts with weights that are, in a mathematical probability sense, extremely unlikely. Oklahoma North (11.1) and Alabama South (12.7) are improbably high in average sentence weights, compared to the U.S. value of 5.9, and they have no counterparts at the low end of the scale. Extreme deviations in relative weight are found in Oklahoma West, Tennessee East, Alabama South, and Iowa South (all much more severe than expected).

Conversely, Alaska, Maine, and Pennsylvania East may be classified as much less severe than expected. The only district with very extreme scores for both average and relative weights is Alabama South, suggesting that sentences are not only severe, but also much more severe than would be predicted on the basis of the offense structure in that district.

The map showing percent placed on probation (Map 6.4) resembles that illustrating average sentence weight; this is to be expected, as probation is a form of sentencing and is figured into average sentence weight. However, there are noteworthy differences in the distributions of probation rates among districts.

Northeastern districts remain most favorable to defendants, but New Mexico through Texas West and South, Louisiana West, Arkansas East, and Minnesota and Wisconsin West are in lower quartiles for probation than for sentence weight. Low probation rates in the central United States correspond with high average sentence weight; there is the same distinguishable belt ranging from the Southwest through North Central to East Coast districts. The South Atlantic districts have considerably higher ranks on percent placed on probation than on average sentence weight. There is also a block of districts in the Mountain and northern Great Plains regions, including Colorado, Utah, and North Dakota, which uses probation relatively heavily.

Relative Use of Probation

The relative use of probation, measuring the difference between the actual and expected proportions of defendants placed on probation, also correlates to some extent with the previously discussed measures. The most prominent feature of Map 6.5 is the block of high-use-of-probation districts in the northwestern quadrant

MAP 6.4: Percentage Placed on Probation

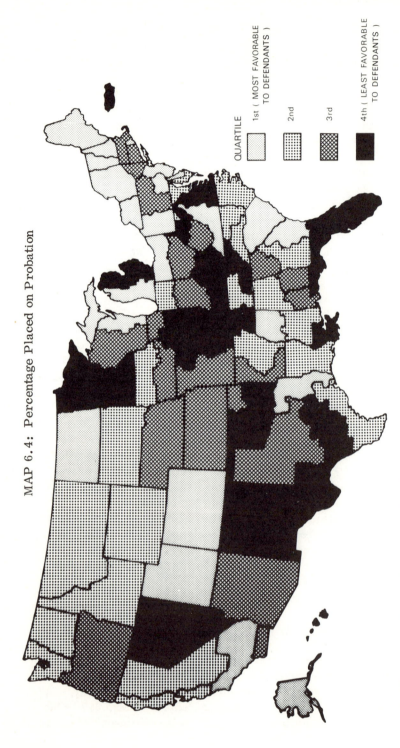

QUARTILE

1st (MOST FAVORABLE
      TO DEFENDANTS)

2nd

3rd

4th (LEAST FAVORABLE
      TO DEFENDANTS)

Source: Adapted from Keith D. Harries and Russell P. Lura, "The Geography of Justice: Sentencing Variations in U.S. Judicial Districts," Judicature 57, no. 9 (1974): 392-401. Data source was: Administrative Office of the U.S. Courts, Federal Offenders in the United States District Courts--1970 (Washington, D.C.: U.S. Government Printing Office, 1972), p. 60.

MAP 6.5: Relative Use of Probation

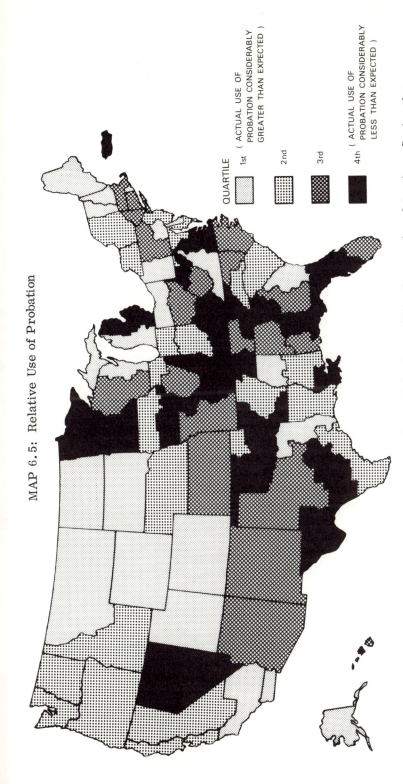

Source: Adapted from Keith D. Harries and Russell P. Lura, "The Geography of Justice: Sentencing Variations in U.S. Judicial Districts," Judicature 57, no. 9 (1974): 392–401. Data source was: Administrative Office of the U.S. Courts, Federal Offenders in the United States District Courts—1970 (Washington, D.C.: U.S. Government Printing Office, 1972), p. 60.

99

of the nation. The by-now familiar pattern of districts least favorable to defendants again reaches from southwestern states to the
center of the East Coast. Alabama and parts of Georgia form a
branch of relatively severe districts reaching into Florida. The
Northeast, California, Texas South to Arkansas East, and several
South Atlantic and upper midwestern districts are again areas relatively favorable to defendants.

Improbably extreme values of percent placed on probation and
of relative use of probation are found in several districts. Maine
(77.4 percent) and Michigan West (78.3 percent) are in the former
category, and Maine and Pennsylvania East in the latter. These
deviations are in the direction of favorability to defendants. At the
other pole of percent placed on probation are West Virginia North
(13.9 percent), Kentucky East (21.5 percent), Florida North (29.6
percent), and Florida Middle (29.5 percent). Minnesota is added to
these when relative use of probation is accounted for.

Map 6.6 generalizes the patterns presented in Maps 6.2
through 6.5, on the basis of geographically contiguous regions. In
general terms, regions I and III tend to be favorable to defendants,
while region II is unfavorable.

This spatial construct was tested using analysis of variance,[10]
and results suggested that the regionalization is reasonably defen-
sible. However, this tripartite classification is not regarded as
rigorous.

Statistical Analysis

In order to take our discussion beyond the descriptive stage,
a simple pilot model was developed based on factors that have previously been suggested as having relevance to sentencing decisions.
The factors utilized are characterized as either legally relevant or
legally irrelevant.[11] The general hypothesis is that only the legally
relevant factors will affect the type and severity of sentences from
place to place. The variables that are legally relevant are as follows.

Characteristics of Defendants. Since recidivists constitute a substantial proportion of criminal defendants, we included measures of
prior police record and prior prison record. It is expected that
districts with large percents on either of these variables will have
more severe sentences.

Distribution of Offenses. The Administrative Office of the U.S.
Courts regards auto theft, narcotics violations, and robbery as the

MAP 6.6: Regions Developed from Overall Rank

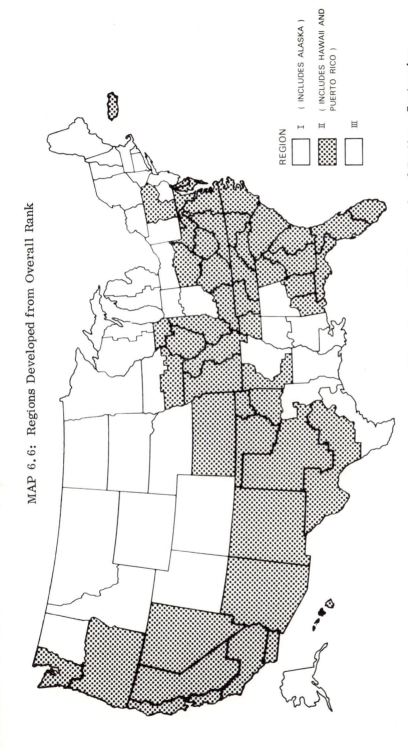

REGION

I   (INCLUDES ALASKA)

II (INCLUDES HAWAII AND
      PUERTO RICO)

III

Source: Adapted from Keith D. Harries and Russell P. Lura, "The Geography of Justice: Sentencing Variations in U.S. Judicial Districts," Judicature 57, no. 9 (1974): 392–401. Data source was: Administrative Office of the U.S. Courts, Federal Offenders in the United States District Courts--1970 (Washington, D.C.: U.S. Government Printing Office, 1972), p. 60.

major serious federal offenses.[12] Theoretically, the greater a
district's percent of these three offenses, the more severe the sentences will be.

Reports of Auxiliary Agencies. Most defendants are the subjects of
presentence reports (70.7 percent in 1970),[13] and some have special observation and study reports (2.5 percent in 1970).[14] While it
is difficult to hypothesize about the effects of presentencing and
special reports, it is likely that those districts with high use of
such procedures would tend to be lower in overall sentence severity.
    The legally irrelevant factors are the following.

Characteristics of Judges. Three variables are included in order to
test the effect of a judge's political affiliation, regional background,
and age on sentence severity. It is commonly accepted that the two
major political parties reflect philosophies of conservatism and
liberalism. Concomitantly, there is the belief, substantiated by
Stuart Nagel,[15] that Democrats are more likely to rule in favor of
defendants than are Republicans. It is hypothesized that districts
with a greater percent of Republican judges will tend to sentence
more severely.
    Two additional measures are concerned with judicial behavior
as a reflection of social background--"degree of southernness," as
measured by Raymond Gastil's southernness index,[16] and age. The
belief that there is a southern personality exists in numerous forms.
The southerner is typified as being violent in nature,[17] strongly
orthodox and fundamental in religion,[18] and politically conservative.[19] These attitudes are felt to contribute to a strong sense of
law and order and to relatively severe sentencing. It was assumed
that age tends to indicate conservatism regardless of political affiliation; older judges are expected to hand down more severe sentences than are their younger counterparts.[20]

Court Procedural Factors. Four measures of procedure were included in the analysis: percent who plead guilty, percent tried by
jury or court, median time to disposition of case, and percent
assigned counsel.
    Each of these variables is considered to be legally irrelevant,
but capable of having an effect on the final disposition of defendants
and on the severity of the sentences. More guilty or nolo contendere
pleas will tend to reduce sentence severity in a district, while more
jury convictions will have the reverse effect. Median time to disposition will tend to have a softening effect on sentences as it increases. Nationally, assignment of counsel tends to mean higher
average sentence weight,[21] and we hypothesize accordingly at the
district level.

For the purpose of this study, a random sample of 30 districts was drawn from the total of 89. Regression analysis was employed to test the hypothesized relationships between the variables described above.[22] The four sentencing measures were related to the 15 legally relevant and irrelevant factors. It was hypothesized that variations in the four sentencing measures would be related only to legally relevant factors. The results of the analysis are presented in abbreviated form in Table 6.2.

TABLE 6.2

Sentencing Measures and Related Variables

Sentencing Measure	Related Variable*	
	Legally Relevant	Legally Irrelevant
Average sentence weight	Observation report (3)	Jury trial (1) Median time (2)
Relative sentence weight	Prior prison record	None significant
Percent placed on probation	Prior prison record (2)	Assigned counsel (1)
Relative use of probation	Prior prison record (1)	Median time (2)

*Numbers in parentheses indicate the rank of the related variables in their importance as statistical explanations of the sentencing variables.

Source: Calculations by authors. The use of the facilities of the Oklahoma State University Computer Center, for computer mapping and statistical analysis, is gratefully acknowledged.

Average sentence weight related most strongly to jury trial, supplemented by another court factor, median time to disposition. The only significant legally relevant variable--observation report-- actually contributed relatively little in a statistical sense.

Only one explanatory measure--prior prison record--was found to account for relative sentence weight, but it did so rather weakly, suggesting that other factors, not considered here, may be more important. One possibility, of course, in relation to both of the sentence weight measures, is the adequacy of the scale of weights, rather than the inadequacy of related factors.

Prior prison record and the assigned-counsel variable were both inversely related to percent placed on probation. Assigned counsel, the legally irrelevant variable, was appreciably more important in the statistical explanation than was prior prison record.

The fourth sentence measurement, relative use of probation, related most strongly (and inversely) to prior prison record, while a weaker (positive) relationship occurred in relation to median time. This finding is apparently contradictory, since median time was, unexpectedly, positively correlated with average sentence weight. More serious offenses may involve long lead times before trial, but the latter may dispose judges toward use of probation; thus both relationships are understandable.

Conclusion

The analysis shows only partial support for the general hypothesis. Prior prison record surfaced as the legally relevant variable that most consistently accounted for variations in sentencing. However, various legally irrelevant factors accounted statistically for significant amounts of variation, and add emphasis to questions being raised about the judicial process.

Interestingly, characteristics of judges did not contribute appreciably to the explanation. Unfortunately, such characteristics became blurred by the necessity of generalizing at the district level, an unacceptably aggregative approach to social behavior that ideally should be observed in a more detailed way.

DRUG SENTENCING IN OKLAHOMA

This section examines patterns of sentencing in Oklahoma, in order to identify their spatial dimensions and attempt to link them to intrastate cultural variations. Since judges and prosecutors in Oklahoma are elected, their actions may be considered to be somewhat attuned to the preferences of the population in each judicial district. It is hypothesized that the eastern and southeastern parts of Oklahoma, colloquially referred to as Little Dixie, may exhibit a pattern of sentencing that differs from that of the rest of the state. The Little Dixie region, which roughly corresponds to the state of Sequoyah proposed in 1905, differs physically and socioeconomically from the rest of the state and provides a framework within which to test a hypothesis relating to regional behavioral differences.[23]

It is suggested that the identification of regional variations in sentencing may have serious policy implications in the administration of the district court system in Oklahoma and in other states in which comparable circumstances may be presumed to exist.

Drug offenses were selected for analysis, partly because public sensitivity to the drug problem is acute, and judges may be expected to be relatively responsive to public mores in their handling of drug cases. Drug sentencing, then, may be a reasonably sensitive indicator of regional variations in judicial behavior.

The Data Base

Source

As noted in Chapter 5, data were gathered directly from court dockets in all 77 Oklahoma counties. Every felony for which the accused actually appeared in court in 1974 was traced through court procedures from initial appearance to appeal, if any (see Chapter 5, Note 8, for the definition of felony in Oklahoma). Potentially, some 52 variables could be recorded for each of 16,211 cases. The data emphasized procedural milestones in each case, rather than the characteristics of defendants, which were not recorded in dockets.[24] The 1,699 drug offenses analyzed here constitute 10.5 percent of the total felonies in 1974 for which an accused appeared in court. * Data were aggregated at the level of the nine adminstrative judicial districts, each of which yielded sufficiently numerous cases to provide an acceptable comparative basis (see Map 6.7).

Definitions of Drug Offenses

The drug offenses dealt with in this analysis are violations of Sections 2-401, 2-402, and 2-509 of the Oklahoma statutes. For purposes of generalization, the various offenses have been reduced to four principal categories: (1) distribution of marijuana or possession of it with intent to distribute; (2) distribution of a controlled drug or possession of it with intent to distribute;[25] (3) possession of a controlled drug or marijuana (second or subsequent offense);[26] (4) cultivation of marijuana.[27]

---

*Complete enumeration (rather than a sampling framework) of all cases was dictated by political considerations relating to the administration of the courts and of the original research. Sampling is not a traditional component of legal research. Thus statistics used in this section describe the universe under consideration; significance levels in tables are provided for the reader's information and are not intended as inferential references.

MAP 6.7: Oklahoma: Administrative Judicial Districts, with Regional Dichotomy Indicated

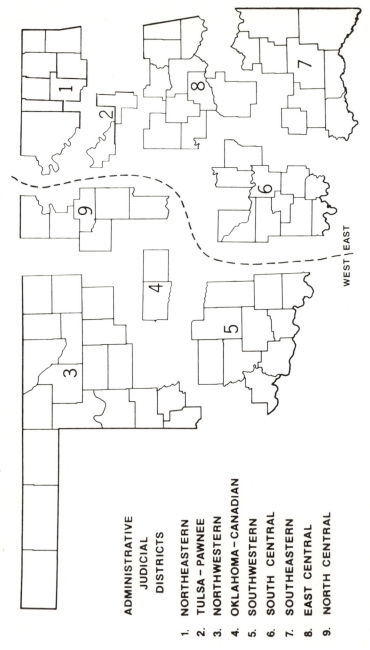

**ADMINISTRATIVE
JUDICIAL
DISTRICTS**

1. NORTHEASTERN
2. TULSA – PAWNEE
3. NORTHWESTERN
4. OKLAHOMA–CANADIAN
5. SOUTHWESTERN
6. SOUTH CENTRAL
7. SOUTHEASTERN
8. EAST CENTRAL
9. NORTH CENTRAL

WEST | EAST

Source: State of Oklahoma, Report on the Judiciary 1969–71 (Oklahoma City: Administrative Office of the Courts, 1973), p. 90.

Analytical Framework

Punishments are standardized through conversion to sentence weights, and regional variations in sentence weights are reviewed and discussed in the context of underlying variations in the regional cultural history of the state.

Prima Facie Regionalization

Considerable evidence exists to suggest a regional dichotomy within Oklahoma, between the Little Dixie or Indian nations area of the east and southeast, and the rest of the state. The former basically corresponds to the region that received the Five Civilized Tribes between about the 1816 and the 1840s. The Chickasaw and Choctaw came mainly from northern Mississippi, the Cherokee and Creek from Alabama and Georgia, and the Seminole from Florida. The northwestern part of the state corresponds to the Oklahoma Territory--the area west of the Indian Nations (see Map 6.8).[28]

There can be little doubt that lifestyles developed differentially in the two Oklahoma regions--northwest and southeast. In the Indian Nations area, for example:

> The Indians formed a sort of caste who owned all
> the land and controlled the political affairs of the
> country. The Whites, who in time came to out-
> number the Indians greatly, could not vote, hold
> office, or own land unless they were intermarried
> citizens; . . . by the census of 1900 there was a
> total population of nearly four hundred thousand,
> only about seventy thousand of whom were Indians.[29]

This southeastern area has historically been characterized by low socioeconomic status: relatively small farms, low values of farm homes, land, buildings, and machinery, a large black population (as well as the highest Indian population), high levels of illiteracy, and low media participation.[30] More recent data confirm the persistence of various pathologies, including relatively high levels of unemployment, welfare, and homicide, and low educational attainment.[31] Another point of contrast between the regions lies in the pattern of European immigration. With the exception of Italian immigrants, who settled heavily in Coal, Pittsburg, and Latimer counties in the southeast (in connection with coal mining employment), most European immigrants located in the northwestern half. Germans were most numerous, constituting 36.5 percent of the foreign-born white population in 1910.[32] It has been suggested that northwestern Oklahoma attracted relatively skilled migrants, while the

MAP 6.8: Oklahoma: The Indian Nations and Oklahoma Territory

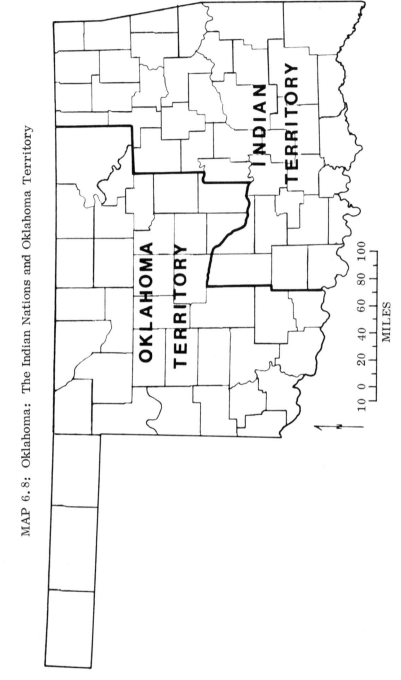

Source: Stephen Jones, Oklahoma Politics in State and Nation, Vol. I (Enid, Okla.: The Haymaker Press, 1974), Map 1, p. 17.

southeast, with its restrictive political and economic structure, tended to be a sink for those who had failed elsewhere.[33]

The distinctive character of organized crime in Oklahoma, with its emphasis on autonomous gangs (colloquially and collectively called the Dixie Mafia) rather than large families of the true Mafia and Cosa Nostra type, further separates southeast from northwest. Assassination-type bombings are common in the east and southeast, and some observers have noted a distinct "Robin Hood syndrome" involving tacit acceptance of violence by the population at large.[34] A connection between organized crime and Italian immigration is probably unwarranted, however, since most Oklahoma immigrants were from northern Italy rather than Sicily, the source of the Mafia.[35]

Another factor to be acknowledged in the proposed regional dichotomy is the intrusion of the "Texas Appalachia" into southern Oklahoma, implied by Terry Jordan.[36] Synthesis of the literature suggests that eastern and southeastern Oklahoma are unlike the rest of the state, yet their cultural history is too complex to allow one simple designation, such as Little Dixie.[37] Stephen Jones has suggested a political-geographical regionalization based on eight areas, and the dichotomy adopted here rests principally on four of those: central Oklahoma, the "Upper east side," Little Dixie, and Tulsa and Washington Counties (see Map 6.9). The dichotomy cuts across the political division between the Republican north and the Democratic south.[38] In terms of Administrative Judicial Districts, the west is composed of Districts Three, Four, Five, and Nine. Districts One, Two, Six, Seven, and Eight are combined to form the east (see Map 6.7).

Attitudinal Expectations

In terms of socioeconomic and lifestyle characteristics, it may be argued that, although culturally complex, the eastern region of Oklahoma is more closely identified with the values of the American South than with those of any other area. There is a considerable literature relating to regional attitudes toward criminal justice questions, and it is possible to build a composite of attitudes toward criminals and, specifically, toward drug offenders, that may be labeled southern.

Compared to other regions, more residents of the South believe that--

crime is to be blamed more on the individual than on society;[39]
they would be more likely to vote for a political candidate who advocates more severe sentencing;[40]
courts deal "about right" with criminals in their region;[41]

MAP 6.9: Regional Dichotomy in the Context of Jones' Political Regions of Oklahoma

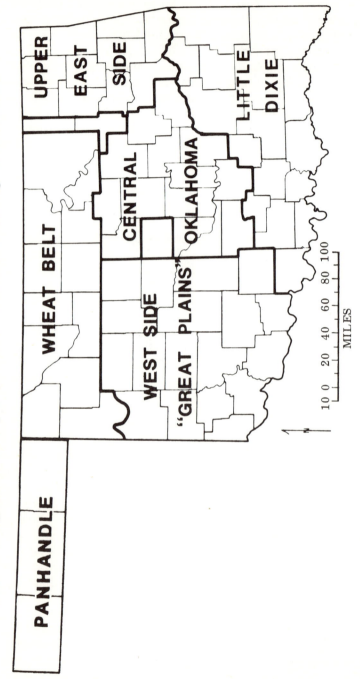

Source: Stephen Jones, Oklahoma Politics in State and Nation, Vol. I (Enid, Okla.: The Haymaker Press, 1974), Map 18, p. 119.

gun-related crimes should not be punished with double sentences;[42]
penalties for use or possession of marijuana should not be reduced,
    and marijuana use should not be legalized;[43]
marijuana is physically addictive.[44]

Furthermore, residents of the South reported the lowest response of any region (7 percent) to the question, "Have you, your-
self, ever happened to try marijuana?"[45]
The southern attitude toward criminals in general, and drug
offenders in particular, may therefore be characterized as tough,
intolerant, and punitive--an expression of the fundamentalist religion of the area.[46] Accordingly, it can be postulated that Oklahoma
East is likely to exhibit harsh sentencing of drug offenders as compared to Oklahoma West.

Sentence Weights

Computational Basis

The basis for the computation of sentence weights is identical
to that discussed in Chapter 5; the reader is referred to Table 5.7.
To recapitulate briefly, deferred and suspended sentences are assigned fixed weights of 0.25. Probation has a weight of 0.25, but
may be multiplied by its quartile value (Q), so that long probations
would receive a weight of 1.00, and short probations 0.25, with the
rest assigned either 0.50 or 0.75. Fines are weighted 1.00 and
multiplied by Q (maximum 4.00), jail terms are weighted 2.00 x Q
(maximum 8.00), and imprisonment is weighted 4.00 x Q for a
maximum of 16.00.

Regional Variation

The overall mean sentence weight is 4.80 (N = 729), with a
standard deviation of 5.84 and a coefficient of variation (CV) of
122 percent).* The weights ranged from a minimum of 0.25 to a
maximum of 20.00, which would be the equivalent of a long prison
term plus a substantial fine.

---

*The coefficient of variation expresses the ratio between the
standard deviation and the mean. If the mean is smaller than the
standard deviation, as it is in this case, the coefficient of variation
exceeds 100 percent. The coefficient provides a useful indication of
the variability of data values. It is expressed as (100 x standard
deviation)/mean.

Regional variation is examined from several perspectives. Initially, mean sentence weights were calculated for each of the four offense categories, by region. These results are presented in Table 6.3. It is immediately apparent that the hypothesized severity of the eastern region is not substantiated. In fact, sentencing is consistently much more lenient in the east than in the west, with the east never constituting more than 67 percent of the mean weight observed in the west in any given category. For the purpose of further explication, the data were rank ordered and dichotomized above and below the median into high and low values, which were then examined in the context of a chi-square table (see Table 6.4). Differences between observed and expected values are substantial in all cells, with the largest contributions to the value of chi-square coming from the smaller-than-expected number of high weights, and the larger-than-expected number of low weights, in the eastern region.

TABLE 6.3

Mean Sentence Weights by Type of Drug Offense and Region

		Weight, by Region	
Offense Category	N	West	East
Distribution of marijuana or possession of it with intent to distribute	310	5.13	2.71
Distribution of a controlled drug or possession of it with intent to distribute	245	8.09	4.39
Possession of a controlled drug or marijuana (second or subsequent offense)	112	5.05	3.36
Cultivation of marijuana	62	1.07	0.68

Source: Authors' computations, based on field data.

In Table 6.5, mean weights are tabulated by mode of punishment. Since deferred and suspended sentences have constant weights, the only source of variation is derived from what may be referred to as combination sentences, with fine, jail, imprisonment, or probation occurring singly or together. The mean for the west is almost a full standard deviation above the overall mean, when the reducing effect of the deferred and suspended sentences is omitted.

It is also notable that the combination weights are less variable in the west (CV = 48 percent) than in the east (CV = 94 percent).

TABLE 6.4

Dichotomized Sentence Weights by Region

Sentence Weight	Region		Total
	West	East	
Low	171.00 (observed)	196.00	367.00
	214.38 (expected)	152.62	367.00
	8.78 (cell chi-square)	12.33	21.10
High	256.00	108.00	364.00
	212.62	151.38	364.00
	8.85	12.43	21.28
Total	427.00	304.00	731.00
	427.00	304.00	731.00
	17.63	24.76	42.38

Note: Chi-square = 42.38 with 1 df and p = 0.0001.
Source: Authors' computations, based on field data.

TABLE 6.5

Mean Sentence Weights by Mode of Punishment and Region

Mode of Punishment	N	Weight, by Region	
		West	East
Fine, jail, imprisonment, probation-- singly or in combination	389	9.88	6.56
Deferred judgment	199	0.25	0.25
Suspended sentence	141	0.25	0.25

Source: Authors' computations, based on field data.

The numerical influence of the two major metropolitan counties (Tulsa and Oklahoma) is so pervasive that it is necessary to examine the idea that what is actually showing up in these statistics is the relative lenience of Tulsa as compared to the harshness of Oklahoma

City, suggested in connection with violent crimes in Chapter 5. In
Table 6.6, weights for combination sentences are disaggregated and
separate means are calculated for Administrative Judicial Districts
Two (Tulsa and Pawnee Counties), Four (Oklahoma and Canadian
Counties), and Seven (nine counties in the southeast approximating
the heart of the Little Dixie area). There is indeed a sharp difference between the metropolitan areas, corresponding to the findings
referred to in Chapter 5. The Little Dixie core area has an intermediate weight, but one based on a very small N. This weight is in
the hypothesized direction of relative severity; overall, however,
the fact that the districts encompassing Tulsa and Oklahoma City
accounted for some 33 percent of all drug felonies probably under-
mines the regional culture model and suggests a paradigm that
would exclude Tulsa and Oklahoma City, and aggregate more categories of cases in order to increase Ns, and consequently increase
the reliability of mean sentence weights. Tulsa appears to be an
enigma in the sense that its sentencing pattern runs counter to the
expectations derived from its cultural context. It has a reputation
as a city with a high quality of life, [47] and it is consistently Republican (having not voted Democratic in either a presidential or guber-
natorial election since 1938). Much of the rest of the eastern area,
on the other hand, is socioeconomically depressed and more likely
to vote Democratic (Bryan County, for example, in the heart of
Little Dixie, has only gone Republican in a presidential or guberna-
torial election once in its history--in the 1972 McGovern-Nixon
contest). It is somewhat surprising that the Republican, and hence
somewhat conservative attitude of Tulsa is not reflected in relative
severity of sentencing. This paradox suggests again the possibly
key role of the prosecutor as discussed in Chapter 5.

The regional dichotomy in sentence weights based on type of
trial yields mixed results (see Table 6.7). The west has the higher
mean weight based on guilty pleas, but there is little difference between the eastern and western regions with respect to jury trials;
in both regions juries are very severe. In terms of the overall
mean and standard deviation, jury sentences in the west are 1.30
standard deviations above the mean, and in the east, 1.51. Jury
trial sentences were less variable in both regions as compared to
pleas or judge trials (CV = 44 percent in both regions). However,
it is recognized that the use of sentence weights tends to have a
statistical smoothing effect in the sense that a harsh sentence--
for example, a long term of imprisonment--will receive a weight
of 16.00, regardless of the fact that it may be the harshest sentence meted out.

TABLE 6.6

Mean Sentence Weights: the Influence of Oklahoma City,
Tulsa, and Nine Southeastern Counties

Mode of Punishment*	Weight, by Counties		
	Oklahoma, Canadian	Tulsa, Pawnee	Nine Southeastern
Fine, jail, imprisonment, probation--singly or in combination	10.96 (N = 158)	6.79 (N = 80)	8.25 (N = 8)

*Deferred judgments and suspended sentences are omitted as
they are constant (0.25).

Note: The nine southeastern counties may be regarded as
substantially approximating the Little Dixie core area as defined in
Map 6.9.

Source: Authors' computations, based on field data.

Table 6.7

Mean Sentence Weight by Type of Trial, by Region

Type of Trial	N	Weight, by Region	
		West	East
Guilty plea	667	5.49	2.06
Jury trial	54	12.35	13.57
Judge trial	8	8.13	15.04

Note: Data are for drug felony offenses.
Source: Authors' computations based on field data.

The differences in sentence weights by mode of attorney appointment are fairly predictable (see Table 6.8). Privately retained
attorneys are likely to be associated with sentences that are lenient
for the region. However, in the west, for both privately and court-
appointed counsel, weights are about twice as high as in the east.

In reviewing the data, one concludes that the best chance for
a lenient sentence in a drug felony case in Oklahoma would be with a

private attorney, and with a negotiated guilty plea in the eastern region--preferably in Tulsa. On the other hand, an undesirable combination of circumstances for the defendant would include court-appointed counsel and a jury or judge trial--least preferably in the west, especially Oklahoma City. The data also suggest the difficulty in fitting sentencing behavior into a general cultural framework. This is not to deny the relationship between regional cultural influences and sentencing behavior. The difficulty is to operationalize the relationship in the context of ecological analysis--small Ns in rural counties, and the general difficulty of data attenuation with increasingly detailed subcategorization, tend to confound intercounty comparisons. The primacy of the metropolitan counties and the desirability of separating their influence from the rest of the state creates further analytical problems. Although the regional variations described do not conform to the cultural model, the differences are nevertheless substantial and adequately demonstrate the existence of undesirable geographical disparities in sentencing. Another possibility is that the specification of Oklahoma's eastern region as conforming closely to the stereotypical South is an unwarranted oversimplification.

TABLE 6.8

Mean Sentence Weight by Mode of Appointment
of Attorney, by Region

| Mode of Appointment | | Weight, by Region | |
of Attorney	N*	West	East
Court appointed	131	8.19	4.21
Retained privately	583	5.58	2.81

*Total number does not equal 729 drug felonies owing to missing data for these variables.
Source: Authors' computations, based on field data.

In the next section, other examples of spatial sentence variation are discussed, with emphasis on Iowa, New York, and California.

SENTENCING VARIATIONS IN OTHER STATES

Iowa

One of the earliest systematic attempts to examine sentencing variation by districts within a particular state was Walter Lunden's analysis of Iowa.[48] Wide disparities were found in the 21 Iowa judicial districts, on the basis of data for a 19-year period, 1935-54. In the imposition of imprisonment, the First District was the highest (37.8 percent), the Thirteenth the lowest (10.2 percent). This amounted to a prison term for each 2.6 cases in District One as compared to one per 9.4 cases in the Thirteenth (see Map 6.10).

The use of jail and fine combinations ranged from a low of 41.4 percent of the cases in District Nine (Des Moines) to a high of 73.4 percent in District Ten (see Map 6.11). Comparable variations were found in relation to dismissals, suspended sentences, bench paroles, and acquittals. Disparity was so rampant that Lunden was prompted to remark:

> When wide disparities in the sentencing practice in courts occur the time appears to have arrived for some better method of judicial administration in order to preserve the social purposes of punishment. If this is not done the very machinery of justice may help to make more criminals.[49]

Disparity was attributed to carrying to extremes the "theories" of "freedom of decision" by judges and by "those who expect a uniform penalty for the same crimes," and it was suggested that

> there appear to be two possible courses of action for the court and for the judge. The first is a complete pre-sentence investigation before the court makes the disposition; the second, is the placing of the sentencing power into the hands of a correctional authority partially separated from the judiciary.[50]

While these were rational suggestions, it appears that disparity is still a problem in jurisdictions or systems in which presentence investigations are used. The suggestion that sentencing be separated from the judiciary underestimated the extent to which judges and court administrators covet power and protect their professional turf, often at the expense of moral equity.[51]

MAP 6.10: Iowa: Percentage of Criminal Court Cases Resulting in Prison Sentences, by Judicial Districts, 1935–54

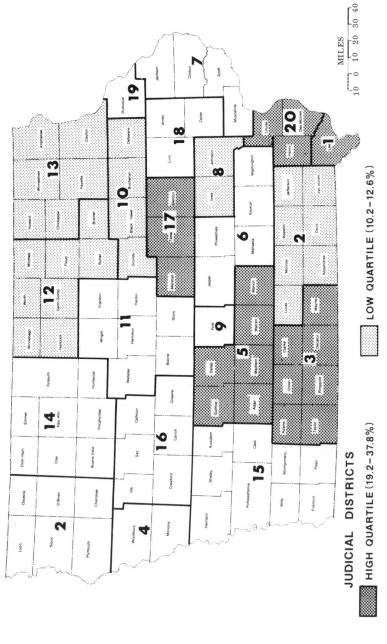

JUDICIAL DISTRICTS

▓ HIGH QUARTILE (19.2–37.8%)

░ LOW QUARTILE (10.2–12.6%)

Note: Map shows extreme quartiles only--state median=16.9 percent.

Source: Adapted from Walter A. Lunden, The Courts and Criminal Justice in Iowa (Ames: Iowa State College, 1957), p. 44.

MAP 6.11: Iowa: Percentage of Criminal Court Cases Resulting in Jail and Fine Sentences, by Judicial Districts, 1935–54

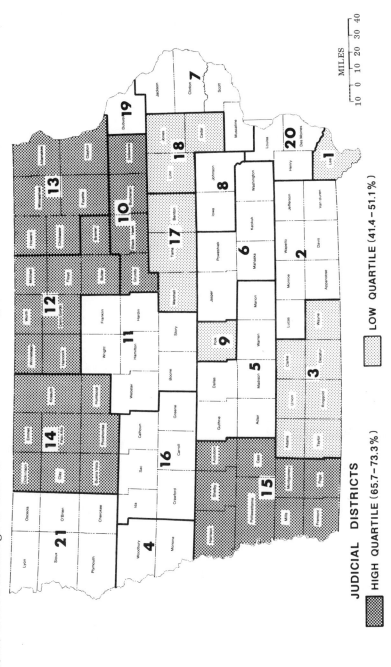

JUDICIAL DISTRICTS

■ HIGH QUARTILE (65.7 – 73.3%)

▨ LOW QUARTILE (41.4 – 51.1%)

MILES
10 0 10 20 30 40

Note: Map shows extreme quartiles only--state median=56.6 percent.
Source: Adapted from Walter A. Lunden, The Courts and Criminal Justice in Iowa (Ames: Iowa State College, 1957), p. 45.

New York

One of the more sophisticated summaries of felony processing available is published by New York State, where a 1973 state law requires regular quarterly reports. (This is in contrast to many states, including Oklahoma, where the emphasis is on the suppression of court data, ostensibly in order to protect judges and court administrators--protection presumably demanded by the incompetent minority.*

County-level geographic detail is generally lacking, but the tripartite division of the state into New York City, suburban New York, and upstate makes some crude areal comparisons possible (see Map 6.12). Variations in felony sentencing, unadjusted for variations in crime patterns, are displayed in Table 6.9. State prison sentences are much more likely in New York City than in suburban New York or upstate. However, this is a reflection of more serious felony crimes in New York City, and cannot be interpreted directly as an expression of sentence disparity. For example, although less than half of all state drug arrests were in New York City in the third quarter of 1974, most of the more serious drug charges were made there. In the city and suburbs, over 75 percent of drug indictments involved sale of controlled substances; upstate the comparable proportion was one-third.

Another aspect of criminal justice that is relatively well documented in New York is judicial processing time. Interestingly, a dismissal or acquittal took twice as long as a conviction in both

---

*In the course of a sentencing research project in Oklahoma, coauthor Harries received a call from the Courts Planner at the State Crime Commission requesting some preliminary aggregate tabulations. These were prepared forthwith and transmitted by phone by 9 a.m. the next day. A call was received later in the day from the court administrator's counsel informing the coauthor that he would be subject to a Supreme Court (of Oklahoma) injunction if the data were released. (The data were paid for with federal funds and consisted of public court docket information.) This is but one of several examples of intimidation of researchers by the courts. Objective analysis of court performance is effectively suppressed in such circumstances--legal redress is essentially impossible in practical terms since district courts are administered by the court administrator who in turn serves at the pleasure of the Chief Justice of the Supreme Court. This suppression of public information by public officials is widespread and constitutes an intolerable breach of societal freedom.

MAP 6.12: New York: Geographic Basis for State Felony Processing

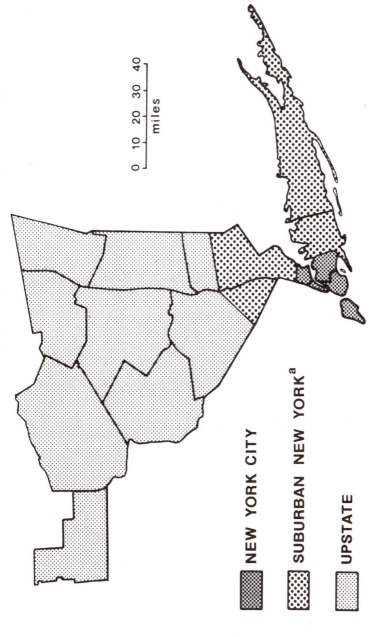

0 10 20 30 40
miles

NEW YORK CITY

SUBURBAN NEW YORK[a]

UPSTATE

[a]Suburban New York consists of Rockland, Westchester, Nassau, and Suffolk counties.
Source: New York State Division of Criminal Justice Services, New York State Felony Processing,
July–September, 1974 (Albany, N.Y.: State of New York, 1974), p. 43.

1974 and 1975. The median time for processing 32,138 dispositions in 1975 was 137 days for the state, 176 days for the city, 147 for the suburbs, and only 91 for upstate. Again, it cannot be said with certainty on the basis of these data that the reported differences in disposition times represent real disparities in processing times. The relative seriousness of crimes in New York City presumably means that cases there tend to be more complex and thus legitimately take longer to dispose of. There are striking differences not only among the three regions, but also between modes of trial (see Table 6.10). Indeed the substantial differences between pleas and trials in all three areas help to convey the pressure for negotiated pleas that in no small part keeps the system afloat everywhere--in spite of strong objections articulated from various quarters, including the National Advisory Commission on Criminal Justice Standards and Goals.[52] New York State is quite typical in its very high proportion of dispositions reached via pleas: New York City reported that 90.6 percent of its convictions came this way; comparable figures were 94.5 percent for the suburbs and 93.6 percent for upstate.

TABLE 6.9

New York State: Geographical Distribution of Sentences
for Felony Indictments Resulting in Conviction,
July–September 1974
(percent of cases)

Sentence	New York City	Suburban New York	Upstate New York	New York State
Unconditional discharge	0.7	0.8	1.6	1.0
Conditional discharge	4.0	2.9	7.3	4.8
Commitment to DACC*	1.6	1.4	0.3	1.2
Probation	39.9	48.9	54.1	45.7
Local prison	9.3	20.1	16.0	13.1
State prison	42.3	23.1	18.6	32.0
Other	2.2	2.8	2.1	2.2
Total	100.0	100.0	100.0	100.0

*Drug Addiction Control Commission.
Source: New York State Division of Criminal Justice Services, New York State Felony Processing, July–September, 1974 (Albany, N.Y.: State of New York, 1974), p. 43.

TABLE 6.10

New York State: Median Days to Conviction,
by Area and Mode of Trial

	Mode of Trial		
Area	Guilty Plea	Jury Trial	Nonjury Trial
New York City	126	315	287
Suburban New York	120	247	392
Upstate	81	173	170

Source: New York State Division of Criminal Justice, New York State Felony Processing, January–December, 1975 (Albany, N. Y.: State of New York, 1976), pp. 60–62.

There is no doubt that New York, like all other states, has its share of sentence disparity and of unequal delays in the disposition of similar cases. However, the official statistics do not provide sufficient geographic detail or case detail to enable convincing documentation of specific inequities.

California

Historically, the leading state in the management of criminal justice data has been California. The Wickersham Commission, in 1931, called for state-level responsibility for crime data, but for many years no significant advance was made apart from the initiation of the Uniform Crime Reports of the FBI in 1931. It is remarkable that as early as 1935, Ronald Beattie suggested a California criminal justice statistics system, with individual reports from the courts as its base. Such a reporting system was created in 1945, and formal legal sanction followed in 1955 with the adoption by California of Thorsten Sellin's model law for uniform criminal statistics (drafted in 1946). Although Pope refers to offender-based transaction statistics (OBTS) as "a new method of improved data collection and reporting,"[53] Beattie points out that "an offender-based reporting system" was begun "in the early stages of developing California criminal statistics."[54] However, it was not possible to begin developing an OBTS system at the arrest stage until 1966, and it is presumably this complete system to which Pope refers.

California sentencing data, then, are relatively abundant; however, the published statistics, as in other states, hardly allow in-depth analysis of sentencing variation on a geographical basis.

A crude analysis of sentence severity based on available data is developed, for 11 counties, in Maps 6.13 and 6.14. In Map 6.13, an approximation of crime seriousness, represented by the percent of arrests in the violence classes used in the FBI crime index, is given in standard deviation categories. Thus Butte County (21.8 percent) was appreciably above the mean of 17.4 percent, Lake (11.4 percent) and Napa (13.1 percent) Counties appreciably below. It would be expected, then, that sentencing severity, expressed in terms of percent of convicted felons going to prison, would mirror this pattern. As Map 6.14 shows, there was an approximation of the prior pattern; Butte County was one of the highest ($Z = 1.1$), Napa the lowest ($Z = 1.4$).* Del Norte County would appear to be a candidate for more detailed disparity analysis; though its violence score was less than one standard deviation above the mean, its prison percent was 2.2 standard deviations above the mean. However, the percent is based on a small N (13), and the descriptive statistics are therefore not very reliable. In fact, prison percents were much smaller in prior years.

In a series of three recent studies, some new insights have been gained on sentencing in California, if only for selected counties, aggregated into a rural/urban dichotomy. The counties, which are unidentified in the studies, appear to be the 12 used earlier by Beattie. Informed guesswork suggests that the urban counties are Sacramento and San Joaquin; the rural are the others shaded in Maps 6.13 and 6.14, with the addition of Plumas.

In the first of the studies the concept of OBTS was introduced and a flow analysis, based on the urban/rural dichotomy, presented. In the rural counties, probation was less likely, jail and prison more likely, as compared to the urban. The second analysis reviewed the problem of sentence disparity and developed a list of independent variables to explain disparity: sex, race, age, prior record, criminal status (whether under criminal commitment), and charge at time of arrest (violent crime, property crime, drug, or other charges). The dependent variables were expressed as probation, jail, or other, for lower courts, with the added category, prison, for superior court dispositions. Some of the urban/rural differences observed included the greater likelihood of urban females

----

*Z-scores express data values in standard deviation units. Thus $Z = 0$ represents the mean, $Z = 1$ represents 1 standard deviation above the mean, and so on.

MAP 6.13: Percentage of Felony Arrests in Index Violence Categories for 11 California Counties, 1971

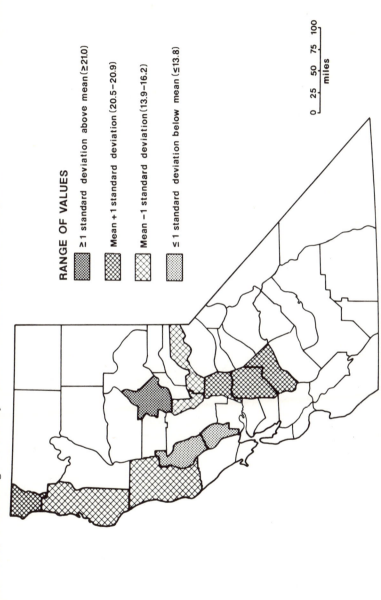

RANGE OF VALUES

≥ 1 standard deviation above mean (≥ 21.0)

Mean + 1 standard deviation (20.5–20.9)

Mean − 1 standard deviation (13.9–16.2)

≤ 1 standard deviation below mean (≤ 13.8)

0 25 50 75 100
miles

Note: Plumas County excluded--data missing for 1971.
Source: Ronald H. Beattie, Offender-Based Criminal Statistics in 12 California Counties (Sacramento:
California Department of Justice, Division of Law Enforcement, Bureau of Criminal Statistics, 1972),
Table IV-B, pp. 32–43.

MAP 6.14: Percentage of Convicted Offenders Sentenced to Prison for 11 California Counties, 1971

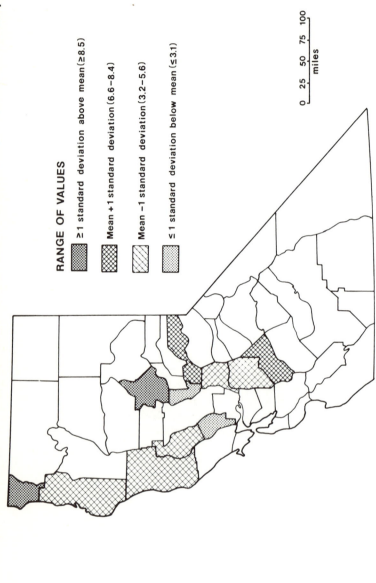

RANGE OF VALUES

≥1 standard deviation above mean (≥8.5)

Mean +1 standard deviation (6.6–8.4)

Mean –1 standard deviation (3.2–5.6)

≤1 standard deviation below mean (≤3.1)

0   25   50   75   100
miles

Note: Plumas County excluded--data missing for 1971.
Source: Ronald H. Beattie, Offender-Based Criminal Statistics in 12 California Counties (Sacramento: California Department of Justice, Division of Law Enforcement, Bureau of Criminal Statistics, 1972), Table IV-A, pp. 20–31.

receiving probation (and avoiding jail), and substantially more severe sentencing of blacks in rural courts.[55] The third analysis
focused specifically on assault and burglary offenders, utilizing
predictive attribute analysis (PAA), a hierarchical approach involving the identification of clusters of variables associated with a particular criterion variable. It was concluded:

> Overall, for both urban and rural areas, the
> highest incarceration rates were associated with
> either having a prior record or being under crim-
> inal commitment and being male. In only one
> instance did race appear in a branching network;
> 70 percent of those urban assault offenders under
> criminal commitment were incarcerated by urban
> lower courts, compared with 59 percent of those
> who were white and under commitment. This
> percentage difference, however, is less than that
> noted for other branches where race was not the
> basis of a split.[56]

While these studies did not have available data on mode of
attorney appointment, bail status, or length of prison sentence,
they are nevertheless indicative of directions that may be taken with
relatively comprehensive transactional statistics.

Other Data on Sentencing Variation

It is, of course, impossible in the course of a brief narrative
to document all the literature containing examples of geographical
variations in sentencing. By way of conclusion, several sources
will be cited so that the interested reader may pursue the topic.
Capital punishment data reveal clearly a heavy southern bias,
in both prisoners under the sentence of death and executions in the
period 1930-75. On December 31, 1975, a total of 283 persons were
under the death sentence in North Carolina, Georgia, Florida,
Louisiana, Texas, and Oklahoma. This was 59 percent of all U.S.
death-row residents; 22 percent of the national total (N = 479) were
in North Carolina. The median age of all prisoners was 26, less
than 2 percent were female, 53 percent were black, 46 percent had
never been married, and most had never finished high school.
Interestingly, black overrepresentation on death row occurred less
in the South than in the other three regions.[57]
Between 1930 and February 1977, 3,860 persons had been
executed under civil authority in the United States. Sixty percent of

these executions occurred in the South; 40 percent were in three states--North Carolina, Georgia, and Texas. Blacks constituted 54 percent of all those put to death, but 89 percent of those executed for rape. All the latter executions were in the South, apart from seven in Missouri.[58] These death sentence and capital punishment distributions are substantially a reflection of historically high homicide rates in the South.[59]

Data on rates of commitment of prisoners to state institutions tend to reinforce the apparently punitive nature of southern justice. Of the 12 states with commitment rates in excess of 100 per 100,000 civilian population in 1974, only two--California and Nevada--were outside the South. The highest rate in the nation was found in North Carolina (207.2 per 100,000).[60] National data on offenses, adjudication, and sentencing are also found in a recent survey of inmates in correctional institutions.[61]

Finally, a couple of whimsical examples of sentencing variation in the United Kingdom are noteworthy. The Times of London published maps showing "Where you can hope to 'get off'--even though you're guilty," "Where the fines are frequent," and "The magistrates who jail." In general, it appeared that (unpaid) magistrates were most punitive in northern counties, least so in various southern and central areas. As in so many other studies, however, seriousness of crime patterns in the various areas was not accounted for.[62] In a similar treatment relating to the enforcement of highway laws, it was pointed out that: "The best place to 'burn old socks' is in Northumberland, where in 1972 only four motorists were prosecuted for having dirty exhaust emissions. But in Hertfordshire, which has about 800 fewer miles of road, the police prosecuted 245 motorists for this offense and issued 72 written warnings."[63]

Again, no attempt was made to account for the various sources of such disparity, which were acknowledged to include variations in police strength, highway mileage, traffic counts, population totals, and so forth. The significance of such articles lies more in their acting as indicators of increasing public sensitivity to inequities, rather than in their substantive contribution to understanding sources of anomaly.

CONCLUSION

None of the studies reviewed in this chapter can be regarded as being completely comprehensive; while significant explanatory variables can be specified, as in Chapter 4, actually assembling these variables in conjunction with complete sentencing data does not appear to have been practicable to date. The various California studies may have come closest to this, but even they have various shortcomings admitted by their authors. In most cases, researchers have had to use available data, and have not normally had the luxury of constructing a data set purely for the purpose of investigating sentence disparity. Where such has been the case, the data have usually been gathered within one jurisdiction and have not lent themselves to spatial comparability.

No institution supports with enthusiasm efforts to undermine its own weaknesses, and courts are no exception. The resistance of the courts to criticism is particularly effective, owing to their immense power; threats from judges or court administrators are likely to be taken seriously. Coauthor Harries's experience in dealing with the Oklahoma courts has been particularly unnerving, and has perhaps created an unfair bias. However, accounts from other jurisdictions suggest that Oklahoma is not entirely unique in this regard. It is sometimes necessary to circumvent the courts in order to obtain court data--from district attorneys, for example, whose data duplicate those of the courts in most respects.

In many cases, then, data inadequacies put the researcher in the position of entering the research process with a hunch, and exiting with the same hunch--which may be better documented, but is generally not confirmed with an acceptable degree of reliability. The gradual improvement of transactionally based criminal justice data systems may alleviate this problem and lead to more definitive future studies on geographically based sentence disparities.

NOTES

1. This section is substantially adapted from Keith D. Harries and Russell P. Lura, "The Geography of Justice: Sentencing Variations in U.S. Judicial Districts," Judicature 57 (1974): 392-401.

2. W. Zumwalt, "The Anarchy of Sentencing in the Federal Courts," Judicature 57 (1973): 96-104.

3. "Agnew case points up inconsistent sentencing for criminal offenses," Wall Street Journal, October 26, 1973, p. 1.

4. See Judicature 60 (1976): 208-32. On television, an ABC special entitled "Justice on Trial" (January 7, 1977) treated the issue of U.S. criminal sentencing. Specifically, federal sentencing was examined on the NBC "Today" show (February 3, 1977).

5. Administrative Office of the U.S. Courts, Federal Offenders in the United States District Courts--1970 (Washington, D.C.: U.S. Government Printing Office, 1972), Table 17, p. 60.

6. Ibid., Table 14, p. 57.

7. For further details, see ibid., Table D11, pp. 130-33.

8. Ibid., Table D-9a, pp. 126-27.

9. Ibid.; Table D-9a contains a complete listing of actual, expected, and relative values, and a more detailed explanatory note.

10. This technique facilitates the testing of the hypothesis that the means of each measurement for each region are significantly different. For further explanation and examples, see Leslie J. King, Statistical Analysis in Geography (Englewood Cliffs, N.J.: Prentice-Hall, 1969), pp. 78-81.

11. This distinction is based in part on discussion by Edward Green in Judicial Attitudes in Sentencing (New York: St. Martin's Press, 1961).

12. Administrative Office of the U.S. Courts, op. cit., Table D-21, pp. 150-51.

13. Ibid.

14. Ibid.

15. Stuart S. Nagel, "Testing Relations between Judicial Characteristics and Judicial Decision-Making," Western Political Quarterly 15 (1962): 425-37.

16. Raymond D. Gastil, "Homicide and a Regional Culture of Violence," American Sociological Review 36 (1971): 412-27. On the basis of judges' law school locations, each judge was assigned a southernness value based on Gastil's index. Our assumption was that a more southern law school would produce relatively severe-sentencing judges.

17. Sheldon Hackney, "Southern Violence," in The History of Violence in America, ed. Hugh D. Graham and Ted R. Gurr (New York: Praeger, 1969), pp. 505-27. See also Keith D. Harries, The Geography of Crime and Justice (New York: McGraw-Hill, 1974), Chapter 2.

18. Ina W. Van Noppen, The South (Princeton, N.J.: D. Van Nostrand, 1958).

19. Robert L. Brandon, "Introduction to 'Southern Democracy,'" in The American South in the Twentieth Century, ed. Robert L. Brandon (New York: Thomas Y. Crowell, 1967), pp. 49-51.

20. Age data were obtained from various Who's Who publications.

21. Administrative Office of the U.S. Courts, op. cit., Table 9a, p. 49.

22. The random sample was stratified by circuits. Regression analysis aids the examination of the nature of relationships between phenomena. See King, op. cit., Chapter 6.

23. Indications of physiographic, sociopolitical, and socioeconomic differences between southeastern Oklahoma and the rest of the state may be obtained from John W. Morris and Edwin C. McReynolds, Historical Atlas of Oklahoma (Norman: University of

Oklahoma Press, 1965), and Meredith F. Burrill, A Socio-Economic Atlas of Oklahoma, Miscellaneous Paper (Stillwater: Oklahoma Agricultural and Mechanical College, Agricultural Experiment Station, 1936).

24. The term "transactional" is currently used to describe data in which the individual offender is the unit of observation. Ideally, transactional data provide a basis for analytically linking the parts of the criminal justice system. See Carl E. Pope, Offender-Based Transaction Statistics: New Directions in Data Collection and Reporting (Washington, D.C.: U.S. Department of Justice, Law Enforcement Assistance Administration, 1975).

25. Categories 1 and 2 are both violations of Sections 2-401, but are separated because, in practice, charges discriminate between offenses involving marijuana and those involving other substances. Nevertheless, the Uniform Controlled Dangerous Substances Act, which is synonymous with the Oklahoma legislation except as amended, places marijuana in Schedule I(C), which lists substances with "high potential for abuse" and "no accepted medical use in the United States," and those that lack "accepted safety for use in treatment under medical supervision" (Oklahoma Statutes Annotated, 63, Sec. 2-203 [1971], pp. 297-300). Penalties for violations in categories 1 and 2 vary from two to 20 years in prison and fines up to $20,000. Subsequent violations invoke double punishment so that a combination of 40 years in prison and a $40,000 fine is possible (Oklahoma Statutes Annotated, 63, Sec. 2-401 [1971], pp. 319-20).

26. A distinction is explicitly made between marijuana and other substances. The pertinent section of the law states that "a second or subsequent violation of this section with respect to any Schedule III, IV or V substance, marijuana or a substance included in subsection D of Section 2-206 is a felony punishable by imprisonment for not less than two (2) nor more than ten (10) years" (Oklahoma Statutes Annotated, 63, Sec. 2-402 [1971], p. 320).

27. Cultivation is prohibited by legislation governing the eradication of "all species of plants from which controlled dangerous substances in Schedules I and II may be derived." Punishment is "a fine . . . not to exceed Fifty Thousand Dollars ($50,000) and imprisonment in the State Penitentiary for not more than ten (10) years. Any person convicted of a second or subsequent violation . . . is punishable by a term of imprisonment twice that otherwise authorized and by twice the fine otherwise authorized" (Oklahoma Statutes Annotated, 63, Sec. 2-509 [1971], pp. 333-34).

28. Morris and McReynolds, op. cit., pp. 13, 50.

29. James Shannon Buchanan and Edward Everett Dale, A History of Oklahoma (Evanston, Ill.: Ron Peterson and Co., 1929), pp. 262-63.

30. Burrill, op. cit., pp. 22, 25, 27, 108-09, 113, 114. Burrill mapped "percentage of families having radios, 1930." Values less than 10 percent were virtually all in the east and southeast. Highest values, about 36 percent, clustered in north central Oklahoma and the Panhandle.

31. Mark M. Miller, Jerry V. Overton, and Keith D. Harries, "The Spatial Delimitation of the Little Dixie Culture Region in Oklahoma" (Paper read at the annual meeting of the Rocky Mountain Social Science Association, Fort Collins, Colo., 1971). Samuel G. Chapman has recently drawn attention to multiple police murders in eastern and southeastern Oklahoma--in Dewar City (Okmulgee County) and Bokchito (Bryan County) (Personal communication with Chapman, September 20, 1976). See his Police Murder and Effective Countermeasures (Santa Cruz, Calif.: Davis Publishing, 1976). Bryan County, in the Southeastern Administrative Judicial District, has also exhibited extremely eccentric judicial behavior, personified by District Judge Sam Sullivan, who was tried by the Oklahoma Court on the Judiciary in July 1976. "Several witnesses testified that he habitually browbeat, harassed and intimidated defendants, lawyers and others appearing before him and conducted court in a bizarre manner. Three persons testified he threatened to kill anyone who attempted to have him disbarred." The prosecutor said, "Little Dixie carries no distinction from any other jurisdiction. It's not enough to say, 'that's the way we do it in Little Dixie'" (Tulsa World, July 31, 1976, p. 1). Sullivan was found guilty of oppression in office and partisan political activities and was removed from office.

32. Douglas Hale, "European Immigrants in Oklahoma: A Survey," The Chronicles of Oklahoma 53 (1975): 179-203.

33. This informal hypothesis was suggested by Hale in the course of private discussion.

34. This point emerged during a panel discussion on organized crime in Oklahoma videotaped for a series, "Issues in Crime and Justice," on September 20, 1976, at the Oklahoma Educational TV Authority, Oklahoma City.

35. Hale, op. cit., p. 196; Marvin E. Wolfgang and Franco Ferracuti, The Subculture of Violence (London: Tavistock Publications, 1967), p. 272.

36. See Terry G. Jordan, "The Texan Appalachia," Annals, Association of American Geographers 60 (1970): 409-27. Jordan's maps suggest the extension of the "Anglo-American hill area" (and its associated culture) into south central Oklahoma.

37. A comparable complexity was encountered by Robert M. Crisler in his effort to identify Missouri's "Little Dixie" in the 1940s. Observers agreed on the inclusion of three core counties,

but were less than unanimous with respect to 18 others (Crisler, "Missouri's 'Little Dixie,'" Missouri Historical Review 42 [1948], pp. 130-39.

38. V. O. Key, Jr., American State Politics: An Introduction (New York: Alfred A. Knopf, 1967), pp. 221-22.

39. Michael J. Hindelang et al., Sourcebook of Criminal Justice Statistics--1974 (Washington, D.C.: U.S. Government Printing Office, 1975), Table 2.15, p. 177.

40. Michael J. Hindelang, Public Opinion Regarding Crime, Criminal Justice and Related Topics (Washington, D.C.: U.S. Government Printing Office, 1975), Table 4, p. 13.

41. Hindelang, Sourcebook of Criminal Justice Statistics--1974, Table 2.71, pp. 204-05.

42. Ibid., Table 2.76, p. 209.

43. Hindelang, Public Opinion Regarding Crime, Criminal Justice and Related Topics, Tables 6 and 7, p. 15.

44. Ibid., Table 9, p. 17.

45. Ibid., Table 11, p. 19.

46. See James R. Shortridge, "Patterns of Religion in the United States," Geographical Review 66 (1976): 420-34.

47. See A. Louis, "The Worst American City," Harper's Magazine 250 (1975): 67-71. This methodologically questionable study rates Tulsa second among the 50 largest cities in the United States. Oklahoma City ranked ninth. Those familiar with both cities generally agree that Tulsa has the higher quality of life.

48. Walter A. Lunden, The Courts and Criminal Justice in Iowa (Ames: Iowa State College, 1957).

49. Ibid., p. 52.

50. Ibid., p. 53.

51. This problem is not peculiar to judges; it seems to be endemic to the legal profession. See Jerold S. Auerbach, Unequal Justice: Lawyers and Social Change in Modern America (New York: Oxford University Press, 1976), pp. 263-306.

52. National Advisory Commission on Criminal Justice Standards and Goals, Courts (Washington, D.C.: U.S. Government Printing Office, 1973), pp. 46-49; this describes Standard 3.1, "Abolition of Plea Negotiation." Plea bargaining has also been discussed in the context of the Attica prison disturbance in New York: "The system . . . results in unequal sentences for the same conduct, depending on whether the inmate is willing or able to strike a good bargain." Paradoxically, in the light of data presented previously in our discussion, the Attica Commission said: "In upstate New York, where court calendars make pressures for plea bargaining less intense, sentences tend to be more severe than in New York City." See New York State Special Commission on Attica, Attica (New York: Bantam Books, 1972), pp. 30-31.

53. Carl E. Pope, Offender-Based Transaction Statistics: New Directions in Data Collection and Reporting (Washington, D.C.: U.S. Government Printing Office, 1975), p. 12.

54. Ronald H. Beattie, Offender-Based Criminal Statistics in 12 California Counties (Sacramento: California Department of Justice, Division of Law Enforcement, Bureau of Criminal Statistics, 1972), pp. 1-4.

55. Carl E. Pope, Sentencing of California Felony Offenders (Washington, D.C.: U.S. Government Printing Office, 1975), pp. 23-24.

56. Carl E. Pope, The Judicial Processing of Assault and Burglary Offenders in Selected California Counties (Washington, D.C.: U.S. Government Printing Office, 1975), p. 28.

57. U.S. Department of Justice, National Criminal Justice Information and Statistics Service, Capital Punishment, 1975 (Washington, D.C.: U.S. Government Printing Office, 1976), pp. 2-3.

58. Ibid., p. 4.

59. For further discussion see Harries, The Geography of Crime and Justice, pp. 30-36.

60. U.S. Department of Justice, National Criminal Justice Information and Statistics Service, Prisoners in State and Federal Institutions on December 31, 1974 (Washington, D.C.: U.S. Government Printing Office, 1976), p. 10.

61. U.S. Department of Justice, National Criminal Justice Information and Statistics Service, Survey of Inmates of State Correctional Facilities, 1974 (Washington, D.C.: U.S. Government Printing Office, 1976), pp. 7-10.

62. Robert Lacey and Jonathan Sale, "Where to Commit Your Crime," The Sunday Times Magazine, January 24, 1971, pp. 8-18. We are indebted to Peter Gillbe of the British Broadcasting Corporation for drawing our attention to this material.

63. Harry Loftus, "Beware the County Crackdown," Drive (British Automobile Association), no. 28 (1974): 74-77. This material was kindly provided by David M. Smith, Professor of Geography at Queen Mary College, London.

7

COURT REFORM AND
REORGANIZATION

Thus far we have dealt with statutes, jury selection, sentencing, and prosecutorial discretion as major ingredients in the study of laws and justice. The only major topic that has not been specifically examined is courts and the court system.[1] The importance of local, state, and federal courts, and the administration of the judicial system has been discussed throughout as being critical in understanding the whys and wherefores of specific cases or concepts. It seems appropriate that the courts be discussed in the concluding chapter as the effectiveness of court administration encompasses all topics previously handled. A further reason for treating it at this point is that any reforms that might be seriously proposed would need to be couched in the framework of the court system. Whether those reforms involve uniform sentencing or similar jury selection procedures at local or state levels, the court system lies at the root of all subjects relating to the administering and delivery of judicial services.

The thrust in this chapter is on geographical dimensions of the court system; that is, how courts have been organized and how they operate. The discussion focuses on the federal court system; what the salient features of the district courts and circuit courts are in terms of certain measures used to examine the court administration. Not only will the present structure and its system be highlighted, but so will specific reforms. Those reforms that are offered relate to the organizational structure of the court system; that is, what kinds of realignments might be necessary and how new judgeships might be allocated to certain districts and circuits. Even though the federal system is studied closely in terms of its geographic character, similar investigations could be carried out in court systems for individual states. Likewise, reforms both

administrative and geographic could be advanced to eliminate ineffi-
cient or ineffective levels in the judicial machinery. That is to say,
the need to scrutinize the court system is essential in society
whether at the federal, state, or local level.

This chapter is divided into four parts. The first presents an
overview of the present status of the court system, which is followed
by a geographic perspective--how a social geographer looks at the
system. Following that, the district and circuit courts are examined
in detail in terms of existing geographical variations. The final part
discusses a number of reforms in court organization, some of which
have been introduced into Senate bills, and others of which might
streamline the federal judiciary machinery. As stated above, the
overall objective of this chapter is to discuss the geography of courts
both in terms of their existing performance and recommendations
for reforming them.

PRESENT STATUS OF COURT SYSTEM

Court systems have come under increased scrutiny in the past
few years. They have been the subject of concern to state legisla-
tors, members of Congress, and various study groups in bar associations. Recent presidents and members of the Supreme Court and
lower courts as well have signaled some of the major problems
facing the American system of justice.[2] They run the gamut from
increased caseloads per judgeship, inadequate pay increases,
lengthy times for disposing of cases, new tiers of courts, merit
selection methods for appointment of judges and peer review panels,
to the methods for removing judges. This list does not include the
numerous criticisms about ideological changes in court philosophy,
or about leniency or strictness in dealing with specific criminal
acts or individuals or bribery. Bringing these issues into public
focus has been instrumental in a number of serious efforts being
studied to improve and streamline the judicial machinery. All too
often in the past, improvement meant making the system more complex. Henry Glick commented on this issue in his succinct treatment of the history of state and local courts:

> Additions to new courts and judges to state judi-
> cial systems generally were not made according
> to any overall plan for the state judiciary.
> Changes were made sporadically and haphazard-
> ly and little attention was paid to the jurisdic-
> tional boundaries of the courts and the possibil-
> ity that the authority of one court might overlap

with that of another. In addition, except for the
power which appellate courts had to review the
decisions of trial courts, each court was an independent institution. Rules of procedure and
decisions themselves varied largely and judicial
decision-making was highly decentralized.[3]

Glick goes on to state that judicial reform has often meant
combining numerous courts with overlapping powers into a more
streamlined system, but that "many states still have highly complex
court systems that have grown gradually over the years. Some
courts have existed for centuries, while others have been added in
more recent times."[4]

TABLE 7.1

State Court Variations

California	Florida
Appellate Courts	
Supreme Court	Supreme Court
District Courts of Appeals	District Courts of Appeals
Trial Courts of General Jurisdiction	
Superior Courts	Circuit Courts
	Court of Record (Escambia County only)
Trial Courts of Limited Jurisdiction	
Municipal Courts	Civil Court of Record
Justice Courts	Criminal Courts of Record
	Civil and Criminal Court of Record
	Courts of Record
	County Judges' Courts
	Juvenile and Domestic Relations Courts
	Small Claims Courts
	Justice Courts
	Municipal Courts
	Metropolitan Court

Source: Henry Robert Glick, "The System of State and Local
Courts," Current History 60 (1971): 342.

Court variations in California and Florida are shown in Table
7.1 to illustrate the diversity that exists. The appellate court and
trial courts are at similar levels, but at the local level the number
of special courts is cumbersome to the administration of justice in
Florida. Glick illustrated this situation with an example from Maryland. "There are no less than 16 different types of courts, with
little uniformity from one community to another. A lawyer from one
county venturing into another is likely to feel as bewildered as if he
had gone into another state with an entirely different system of
courts."[5]

In spite of the problems arising due to geography or administration, there have been reforms in the past few years.[6] Voter approval of necessary changes has been forthcoming and the passage
of necessary congressional legislation seems likely. Three examples
illustrate that the climate for change exists. First, in November
1976 voters in a number of states (Connecticut, Florida, Maryland,
Missouri, Nevada, New York, and North Dakota) approved methods
that were instrumental in bringing much needed court reform.[7]
Second, Congress has held hearings and has had legislation introduced that would realign the circuit courts and assign new judgeships; specific geographic and judicial personnel recommendations
are part of the bills.[8] Third, Chief Justice Warren Burger has publicly echoed many problems facing the court system nationwide and
particularly the federal system.[9] His reports on the state of the
judiciary have served not only to underscore the severity of management problems facing courts, but to prod Congress and other
legislative bodies charged with administrating courts to recommend
and institute sorely needed reforms.

GEOGRAPHIC PERSPECTIVE ON THE COURT SYSTEM

The administration of courts can be examined in one of two
ways, either in terms of vertical or horizontal dimensions. A vertical analysis would encompass a discussion on the different layers
of the court system from local to state to federal. Each layer per-
forms a particular type or set of judicial functions that are integrated
into subsequently higher levels of the judicial hierarchy. A horizontal discussion of the court system would consider the geographical or
areal patterns of the different elements and determine how they are
tied into a set of units at state or federal levels.[10] Treatments of
the courts and court system in a vertical sense are best reserved
for those familiar with the responsibilities of the different levels
and how effective they each are, individually and collectively, in
meeting the rights of citizens and groups and in protecting society

from unwarranted and unjust delays or judicial processes. Those students of law and local, state, and federal government, and those familiar with the interfaces between the different levels, are in the best position to evaluate the existing system and advance proposals for reform. The horizontal dimensions of the court system, or a geographic perspective, may have been unintentionally overlooked or not considered seriously as being a valuable way to consider possible changes.

The geographic or spatial perspective on the court systems is basically one of organization. The major questions social geographers would ask are the following: How was the system organized (in an areal or horizontal sense)? What were the overriding criteria used to determine the numbers, size, and shapes of the different areal or geographic units (for example, U.S. district courts or circuit courts)? When were the boundaries and areal units established? How effective are the areal units in the different systems functioning today? And finally, is the judicial machinery operating satisfactorily at present in all parts of a region (state or section of the nation) or are reforms needed? The geographic queries raised relate to the ways in which a state or the federal government has organized space to meet judicial responsibilities. A political organization of space that attempts to meet the judicial needs of society would be different from that where representatives are elected or human services such as education, police, or welfare administration are handled.

The organization of space involves a process of delimiting regions and assigning or allocating individuals, in this case judges, to those regions. The regions are functional in character; that is, they are responsible for performing or delivering a particular service to the population identified by the assigned boundaries. Regions are areas of some expressed homogeneity; they may be delimited on the basis of economic activities (an agriculture or industry base), demographic character (a rural or urban setting), social/political heritage (ethnic stock, racial group, or philosophical outlook). Regions are homogeneous if for no other reason than that the spatial mix in each is distinct from all others. Regions that are organized for judicial services are all alike in that all parts of each, whether adjacent to contiguous units or at the center, are affected by what happens throughout the entire region. The administration of a court in essence covers all segments within a bounded or organized space.

Boundaries are essential and necessary parts of organizing space.[11] They are not national or superimposed on the physical or cultural landscape by God or any supernatural being. Rather, they are human-made. Each boundary identified and each spatial unit established evolved as a result of human decisions. If boundaries are drawn along parallels and meridians or along mountain crests or river courses, some individual or group with a geographic perspective on space organized them. In a social and political context the organization of space has been accomplished in many different ways. It depended on who was performing the organization in terms of the actual reasoning for boundary drawing and the number of units identified. Regions used to establish court systems may have been determined by using existing county boundaries and state boundaries, the rationale used for delimiting U.S. district courts and circuit courts. Those counties assembled into regions within a state may have been grouped to include those with some underlying similarity. Possibly they had equal populations or homogeneous agricultural orientation or a similar underlying ethnic/racial tradition or a philosophical outlook in common. These may have also been used to group states into a given circuit court. The point made here is that some understanding of geography or of space and spatial variations was used to decide on the method of regionalization, the boundaries, the number of areal units, and the internal character of each unit.

A social geographic investigation into the organization of the court system at present would determine if indeed spatial variations exist in terms of a number of statistical measures or criteria available that ascertain court performance. It would call for looking at the population sizes of court districts, the judgeship/population ratio, the caseload per judgeship, and the length of time for disposing of individual cases. These parameters would be used to discuss the existing statistical surfaces of the court system. If contrasts appear, attempts should be made to ferret out the reasons for those areal differences. Such an analysis could be performed at state levels or within a particular section such as New England or the Southwest, or for the entire nation.

Insights into the effectiveness of a system can be gained by analyzing the present situation. These are often most useful to identify flaws that have needed correction. Advancing corrective measures or reforms can only be posited after the present situation has been demonstrated to have weaknesses of such magnitude that the entire system is in jeopardy. Geographic discussions of court reform are based on the way the present system evolved and on the realization and observation (cartographically) that substantial variations exist. Court reforms in a geographical context call for a reorganization of space: How might the spaces for administering the judicial machinery be organized to meet its responsibilities and obligations to society? Legitimate questions that may be raised are the following: Are new regions or groupings of units needed? What criteria might be used for regrouping? Are new criteria needed that were not considered previously? What importance is attached

to boundaries today? Is the social, economic, and political significance of boundaries different from when the present court organization was established? And how many areal units are feasible both
from an administrative perspective and from that of performing and
delivering judicial services?

It becomes apparent in discussing reforms that the geographic
and legal-administrative spheres overlap. Reforming the judicial
administrative machinery may even call for a consideration of new
challenges to lawyers, judges, legislatures, and all political units
(townships, counties, cities, and states themselves). Perhaps to
achieve certain goals in court management and administration, there
will need to be ideas contemplated and proposals advanced that are
counter to the existing organization (vertical and horizontal). Much
depends on the severity of existing problems, the goals of a system,
and the willingness to diligently pursue genuine reforms in a geographic and nongeographic fashion.

The discussion in the remainder of this chapter is divided into
two sections--one that treats the existing picture of the spatial variations in the U.S. district courts and the circuit courts, and one that
puts forward a number of reforms, some of which have already been
seriously considered. The focus on a court system could be on any
level--local, state, or federal. The reason for focusing on the
geography of court administration at the federal level is that it is
the best level from which to examine the system and its problems in
a national context. To correct any wrinkles or serious flaws in the
district or circuit courts would affect not only the federal government but its dealings with individual states or groups of states as well.

GEOGRAPHIC DIVERSITY AND COMPLEXITY

The following discussion on the U.S. district courts and circuit courts examines variation in terms of several criteria: the
total population of a district or circuit, population per judgeship,
the number of filings and the number of filings per judgeship, the
number of pending cases per judgeship, the weighted filings per
judgeship, and the median time--in months--from the filing of a
complete record to the disposition of civil cases.[12] These are
looked at both cartographically and statistically.

In 1976 there were 399 district court judgeships that were assigned to the 50 states and the District of Columbia, and to Puerto
Rico, Guam, the Virgin Islands, and the Canal Zone. They were
distributed in numbers roughly equal to the population distribution
of the nation, with the largest number being in and around the major
metropolitan areas (see Map 7.1). The largest number were

MAP 7.1: District Judgeships, 1976

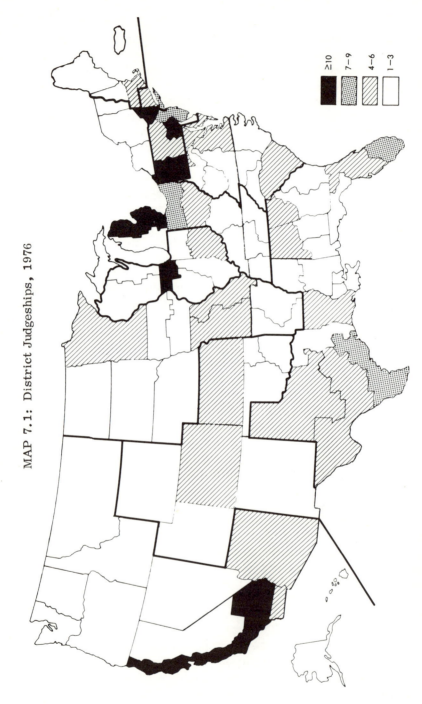

≥10
7–9
4–6
1–3

Source: Director of the Administrative Office of the U.S. Courts, Management Statistics for United States Courts, 1976 (Washington, D.C.: U.S. Government Printing Office, 1976).

assigned to the New York Southern District (27); Pennsylvania,
Eastern (19); California, Central (16); Illinois (13); Michigan, Eastern (10); and Pennsylvania, Western (10). These six districts included New York City, Philadelphia, Los Angeles, Chicago, Pitts-
burgh, and Detroit.

A number of interrelated measures are considered to reflect
court performance and caseload per judgeship. It is expected that
measured on a nationwide basis, for 89 district courts, there would
be a positive relationship between the total population and total filings, between the filings per judgeship and the population per judgeship, and between the total filings and the population per judgeship.

Since there is little agreement between several of these criteria that might be used to evaluate court administration and the performance for judgeships on a district basis, it is not surprising that
the cartographic patterns also defy a simple explanation that is either
comprehensive or regionalizes in light of social or economic character of sections of the nation or parts of a state. If the 89 districts
and the territories are considered in terms of their 1970 total population, the smallest are the Canal Zone with nearly 45,000, the
Virgin Islands with 63,000, and Guam with 87,000. Outside these
territories the smallest districts are those with only one or two
judgeships; that is, the Alaska District (300,000), Wyoming (332,000),
Vermont (444,000), and Nevada (489,000). The largest districts in
total population are California, Central (10.3 million); New York,
Eastern (8.9 million); Illinois, Northern (7.6 million); and New Jersey
(7.1 million). Five others exceeded 5 million, and 30 were between
2 and 5 million. The largest populations were for those districts
that included the largest cities.

The population per judgeship averaged slightly over 500,000
for all districts. However, this figure was virtually meaningless
when all districts were considered cartographically (see Map 7.2).
Three districts had less than one judgeship per 100,000 population;
these were the Canal Zone, Guam, and the Virgin Islands. Four
more had less than one per 200,000 population: New York, Southern;
Delaware; Louisiana, Eastern and Middle; and Alaska. Three districts that had a ratio near the national median were Alabama,
Northern; Virginia, Eastern; and Kentucky, Western. At the oppo-
site end of the spectrum five districts had one judgeship representing more than 1 million: Illinois, Southern; California, Eastern;
Michigan, Western; New York, Northern; and Wisconsin, Western.
The Wisconsin Western District has 1.6 million population, more
than three times the national average population per district and
over 50 times that of the population for the Virgin Islands. As Map
7.2 reveals, there is often little uniformity to the ratio either on a
regional or statewide basis. The New York Southern District has

MAP 7.2: Judgeship/Population Ratio

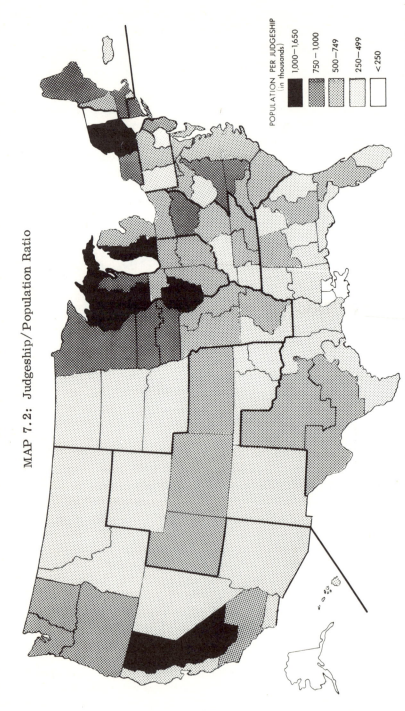

POPULATION PER JUDGESHIP
(in thousands)

1,000–1,650
750–1,000
500–749
250–499
<250

Sources: Director of the Administrative Office of the U.S. Courts, Management Statistics for United States Courts, 1976 (Washington, D.C.: U.S. Government Printing Office, 1976), and U.S. Department of Commerce, Bureau of the Census, 1970 Census of Population (Washington, D.C.: U.S. Government Printing Office, 1970).

27 judgeships serving 3.3 million, with an average of 125,000 population per judgeship. The New York Northern District has two judgeships serving 2.9 million, or 1.46 million per individual judgeship.
Similar striking contrasts exist in Michigan, California, Illinois,
and Wisconsin. In states with more than one district the districts
most nearly equal in the judgeship/population ratio are in Mississippi,
Iowa, and Oklahoma.

During 1976, for those district courts for which data are available, there were nearly 137,000 cases filed. The largest number of
filings were in New York, Southern (7,722); California, Central
(5,962); and Illinois, Northern (5,413). In general the largest total
filings were directly related to total population (see Map 7.3). Outside the territorial possessions, the lowest totals were in sparsely
populated rural districts, North Dakota (326), Vermont (343), Maine
(356), and Wyoming (351). Alaska had more filings than anticipated,
possibly due to the population increase associated with the Alaskan
pipeline construction and lure to the frontier; its total nearly equaled
that of Illinois, Southern, even though this Illinois district had over
three times the population of Alaska. The number of filings per
judgeship averaged 341 nationwide. The most filings per judgeship
were not in the districts with the most filings (see Map 7.4). The
Georgia, Southern caseload per judgeship was 1,182; the caseload
for the Virgin Islands was 1,173, and for the Virginia Western District, 1,008 filings. The North Dakota filings per judgeship were
the lowest (163), outside of Guam, with Vermont (172) and Delaware
(202) the next lowest. On a nationwide basis the districts with the
heaviest filings had seven times those with the lightest number.

The business of district court proceedings can be measured
statistically and cartographically by using two indicators: the number of pending cases per judgeship, and the period of wait from the
filing of a complete record to the disposition of civil cases. In 1976
the pending cases per judgeship for all district courts ranged from a
high of 2,100 cases in Massachusetts to 104 in North Dakota. Nationwide there appeared to be little consistency from district to district,
from state to state, or even from circuit to circuit (see Map 7.5).
The nationwide average was 311 cases per judgeship. The West
Virginia Southern averaged 1,254 cases per judgeship while the West
Virginia Northern averaged 441 cases. The Florida Central value
was more than three times that of Florida, Northern. The high number of pending cases per judgeship in Massachusetts was not charac-
teristic of the other New England states; it exceeded almost seven-
fold that of Maine, New Hampshire, and Rhode Island, and by over
ten times that of Vermont. The median wait in disposition of cases
ranged from one month in Louisiana, Eastern, and the Canal Zone
to more than two years in Arizona; Michigan, Western; Massachusetts;

MAP 7.3: Total Cases Filed, U.S. District Courts, 1976

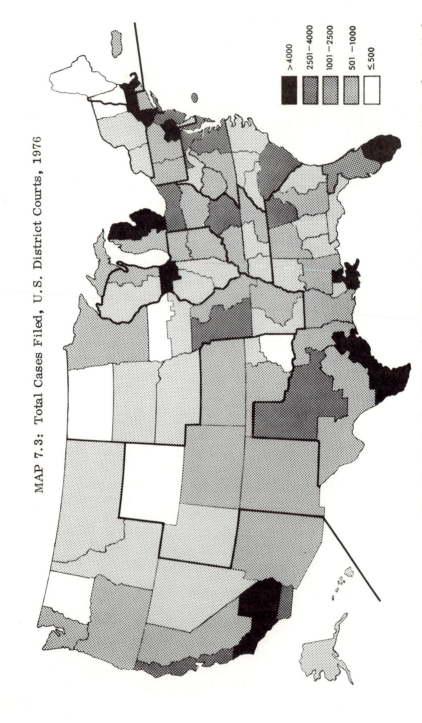

>4000
2501–4000
1001–2500
501–1000
≤500

Source: Director of the Administrative Office of the U.S. Courts, Management Statistics for United States Courts, 1976 (Washington, D.C.: U.S. Government Printing Office, 1976).

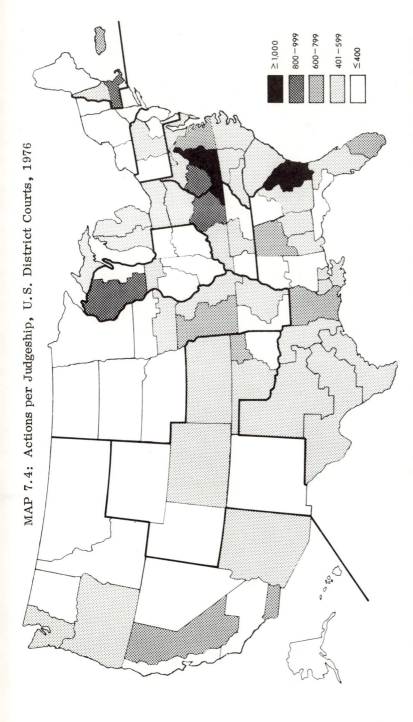

MAP 7.4: Actions per Judgeship, U.S. District Courts, 1976

≥ 1,000
800−999
600−799
401−599
≤400

Source: Director of the Administrative Office of the U.S. Courts, Management Statistics for United States Courts, 1976 (Washington, D.C.: U.S. Government Printing Office, 1976).

MAP 7.5: Cases Pending per Judgeship, U.S. District Courts, 1976

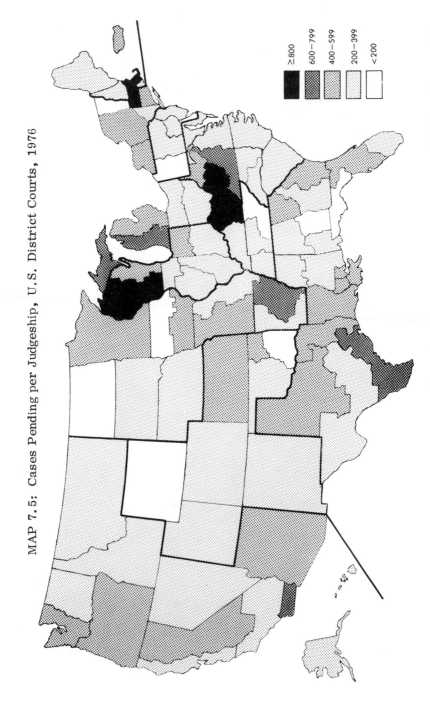

≥800
600—799
400—599
200—399
<200

Source: Director of the Administrative Office of the U.S. Courts, Management Statistics for United States Courts, 1976 (Washington, D.C.: U.S. Government Printing Office, 1976).

and Wisconsin, Eastern (see Map 7.6). In the last two districts the
median length was 29 months. For most districts reporting, the
cases were disposed of in less than 12 months. Eleven months was
the national average for districts reporting 1976 data. On a state
basis the location where the case was filed may have had a great
deal to do with the time involved from initial filing to final disposition. In Texas, Eastern the median time was 5 months; in Texas,
Northern, 9 months; in Texas, Western, 13 months; and in Texas,
Southern the time was 18 months. State averages ranged widely even
within a region, as in New Mexico (3 months) and Arizona (25 months).

A partial reason for the delays in disposing of cases and the
number of cases pending per judgeship may be explained by the severity of the civil and criminal cases filed in the district courts. A
rough index to the types of cases is provided in what the Administrative Office of the U.S. Courts calls the weighted filings. It is an index developed in 1969 and used since in annual official published
statistics to weigh the types of civil and criminal cases considered.
The civil and criminal filings are weighted according to those that
are lighter than average, those that are average, and those heavier
than average (see Table 7.2). On a nationwide basis the weighted
filings per judgeship also had little uniformity (see Map 7.7). The
median value for the nation was 307. The highest values could not
readily be associated with the largest populated districts, the most
urban, or the most rural. High and low filings existed in all settings.
The highest values were in Virginia, Western (905); Georgia, Southern (843); Wisconsin, Western (817); and Massachusetts (810). The
lowest tended to be in very rural districts, North Dakota (157) and
Vermont (179), but not entirely as some urban districts were next,
Delaware (217) and Pennsylvania, Western (217). The values per
district often varied considerably from one district to another, even
within the same state, as in Wisconsin, Eastern (353), and Wisconsin,
Western (817), or as in Oklahoma, Northern (643), Oklahoma, Western (482), and Oklahoma, Eastern (282). Large metropolitan areas
also were far from uniform, as in New York, Eastern (416), covering New York City; California, Central (662), covering Los Angeles;
Illinois, Northern (496), covering Chicago, and Pennsylvania,
Eastern (277), covering Philadelphia.

The lack of uniform patterns at the regional or national levels
is further apparent in reviewing selected measures. It is expected
that in using the 89 district courts as the areal unit there would be
positive and direct relationships between a number of variables (see
Table 7.3). However, for most variables this is not shown to be the
case. There is a high positive relationship between the total number
of filings and the total population of a district; this is not surprising.

MAP 7.6: Median Time from Filing to Disposition, 1976
(in months)

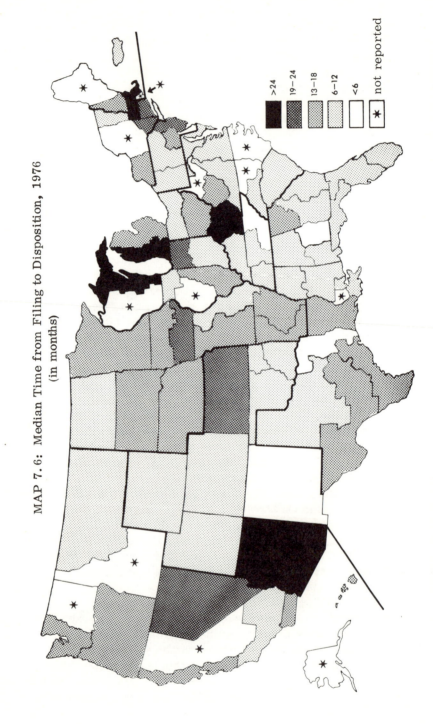

>24
19—24
13—18
6—12
<6
not reported

Source: Director of the Administrative Office of the U.S. Courts, Management Statistics for United States Courts, 1976 (Washington, D.C.: U.S. Government Printing Office, 1976).

MAP 7.7: Weighted Filings per Judgeship, U.S. District Courts, 1976

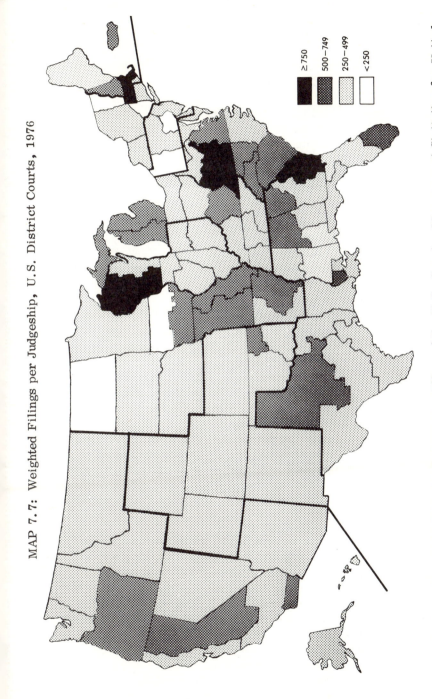

≥ 750

500 − 749

250 − 499

< 250

Source: Director of the Administrative Office of the U.S. Courts, Management Statistics for United
States Courts, 1976 (Washington, D.C.: U.S. Government Printing Office, 1976).

TABLE 7.2

Classification of Cases Used to Calculate Weighted Index

Case Class	Civil	Criminal
Lighter than average	NARA* and Social Security Commerce (Interstate Commerce Commission) Prisoner petitions Forfeitures and penalties and tax suits	Immigration Embezzlement Auto theft Weapons and firearms
Average	Real property Labor suits Contracts Torts	Selective Service Liquor, Internal Revenue Burglary and larceny Drug laws
Heavier than average	Copyrights, patents, and trademarks Civil rights Antitrust	Forgery and counterfeiting Fraud Homicide, robbery, assault and sex offenses

*Narcotic Addict Rehabilitation Act.

Source: Director of the Administrative Office of the U.S. Courts, Management Statistics for United States Courts, 1976 (Washington, D.C.: U.S. Government Printing Office, 1976), p. 127.

The correlations for a number of other variables--between the number of actions per judgeship and the population/judgeship ratio, between the number of pending cases in the districts and their total population, and between the total number of judges and the total population--all approach zero. The lack of any direct relationship, when one is expected, further demonstrates the complexity of the present state of the district court system. There were district courts with few and with many pending cases in large and small populated districts, as well as districts not varied in population/judgeship ratio but with few or with many actions per judgeship. Aside from one rather moderately high correlation between total filings and total

population, the only other positive correlation was between the number of judgeships per district and the total population. Even on the
scatter diagrams showing these relationships, there were still
anomalous districts. In short, at the district court level, diversity
and complexity were evident both cartographically and statistically.

TABLE 7.3

Hypothesized and Statistical Relationships for Selected
Variables Relating to District Courts

Variables		Hypothesized	Coefficient of
Dependant	Independent	Relationship	Correlation (r)
Total filings	Total population	+	.87
Filings per judge	Population per judge	+	.01
Total filings	Population per judge	+	.71
Total pending cases	Total population	+	.01
Total number of judges	Total population	+	-.21

Sources: U.S. Department of Commerce, Bureau of the Census, 1970 Census of Population (Washington, D.C.: U.S. Government Printing Office, 1970), and Director of the Administrative
Office of the U.S. Courts, Management Statistics for United States
Courts, 1976 (Washington, D.C.: U.S. Government Printing Office,
1976).

The nine U.S. court circuits and the District of Columbia,
with 97 judgeships, serve the nation's nearly 215 million population
in the 50 states as well as Puerto Rico, Guam, the Virgin Islands,
and the Canal Zone. In 1976 there were 18,408 cases filed in all
courts of appeals, an increase of 10.5 percent over 1975 and 44 percent since 1971. There have been no additional judgeships created
during this period, which would explain the number of appeals filed
per judge increasing from 132 in 1971 to 190 in 1976. The number
of pending appeals per judgeship increased during this same six-
year period from 95 to 145.

On a regional (court circuit) basis the geographic and administrative variations were considerable. In population alone, not

counting the 757,000 in the District of Columbia, the figures ranged from 31.8 million and 30.3 million in the Fifth and Ninth Circuits, respectively, to 8.4 million in the First (see Table 7.4). The number of states within each ranged from three in both the Second and Third Circuits to seven in the Eighth and nine in the Ninth. The population per judgeship ranged from a high of 2.9 million in the Sixth to 1.2 million in the Tenth. The nation's 73 percent urban population is not matched for all circuit courts. The percent urban is over 83 percent in the Second and Ninth Circuits and lowest in the Eighth (only 54 percent). The number of cases filed ranged from over 3,600 in the Fifth Circuit and 2,900 in the Ninth Circuit to only 564 in the First Circuit. The number of actions or appeals per judgeship was heaviest in the Fifth and Ninth Circuits and lightest in the Tenth and Eighth. The number of pending appeals per judgeship tended to correspond with the total actions. The median time period from filing a complete record to its disposition was nearly one year in the District of Columbia and 11 months in the Ninth Circuit, and less than five months in the Eighth Circuit.

CHANGES AND REFORMS

Changes in the federal court system have been evident since the writing and passage of the Constitution. Article III, Section I stipulates: "The judicial power of the United States shall be vested in the Supreme Court, and in such inferior courts as the Congress may from time to time ordain to establish."

The administrative foundation for the federal courts was laid out in the Judiciary Act of 1789.[13] It divided the nation into three circuits, Southern, Middle, and Eastern; the boundaries corresponded with state boundaries and, in the words of Peter Fish, "thus opened the courts to state and sectional influences and practices."[14] As the nation grew in territory and later in states, new circuits were created. From the original three circuits the number grew to six in 1804, nine in 1866, and ten in 1929. The District of Columbia was created by Congress in 1893. The 11 circuits thus have remained intact for nearly 50 years.

District courts were also provided in the 1789 act when the 11 states were divided into 13 districts. Each state was organized into a single district except Massachusetts and Virginia, which both received an additional one. Throughout most of the last century districts were added as states were admitted and their population grew.[15] Most had at least two, as they still do, except those largest in population. The number has increased from 13 in 1789 to the current total of 89 district courts. If the District of Columbia and the territories

TABLE 7.4

Selected Data on Courts of Appeals, 1976

Data	Court Circuit										
	First	Second	Third	Fourth	Fifth	Sixth	Seventh	Eighth	Ninth	Tenth	District of Columbia
Total filings	564	1,898	1,621	1,464	3,629	1,628	1,247	1,080	2,907	1,110	1,260
Total terminations	482	1,947	1,439	1,336	3,149	1,396	1,138	987	2,575	863	1,114
Total pending	307	793	1,033	1,178	2,885	1,145	895	592	2,968	963	1,351
Percent prosecuted in filings (1975–76)	18.2	9.1	16.5	11.0	10.2	13.4	6.6	7.0	6.4	13.3	13.2
Percent prosecuted in filings (1971–76)	47.3	33.4	47.4	20.9	56.7	60.4	38.2	51.5	50.2	51.2	19.4
Number of judgeships	3	9	9	7	15	9	8	8	13	7	9
Appeals filed per judgeship	188	211	180	209	242	181	156	135	224	159	140
Pending appeals per judgeship	102	88	115	168	192	127	112	74	228	138	150
Total appeals terminated per judgeship	161	216	160	191	210	155	142	123	198	123	124
Opinions signed per judgeship	59	45	30	47	52	27	41	44	33	43	24
Median time (months) from filing complete record to disposition	5.3	5.2	6.4	9.0	6.0	7.2	7.0	4.7	11.1	9.4	11.9
Total population (1970) in millions	8.4	21.7	19.5	17.9	31.9	26.7	20.7	18.0	30.3	9.5	.7
Percent urban	78.3	83.0	77.9	56.3	70.8	69.6	74.8	53.8	83.7	71.0	100.0
Judgeship/population ratio (in millions)	2.7	2.3	2.1	2.5	2.1	2.9	2.5	2.2	2.6	1.2	--*

*Does not apply--less than one million population.

Sources: Director of the Administrative Office of the U.S. Courts, Management Statistics for United States Courts, 1976 (Washington, D.C.: U.S. Government Printing Office, 1976), p. 12; U.S. Department of Commerce, Bureau of the Census, 1970 Census of Population (Washington, D.C.: U.S. Government Printing Office, 1970).

of Guam, the Virgin Islands, and the Canal Zone are added, the
number is 93. The number has not changed since 1968.

The present geographical delimitation for district courts is
codified in legislation passed by Congress in 1911; Senate Bill 7031
and House Resolution 23377 were designed "to codify, revise, and
amend the laws relating to the Judiciary." The ensuing statutes
identified the names of the districts (if more than one) within each
state, the counties to be included in each, and the place where cases
would be heard. While the judicial machinery, from a geographical
point of view, in large part rests on the creation of Public Law 475
(of 1911), from a legal viewpoint the Court of Appeals Act of 1891
is significant. In order to facilitate the prompt disposition of cases
and to relieve the Supreme Court of involvement in general litigation
in the circuit courts, legislation provided for a new circuit court of
appeals that had intermediate jurisdictional responsibilities of an
appellate nature. The appellate jurisdiction of the old circuit courts
was gradually terminated as were the Supreme Court duties at the
circuit level.

Thus the past two centuries of judicial history reveal that
there have been changes and reforms instituted to provide for a
more effective and smooth-running judicial machinery. Since the
stress in this chapter has been on the present status of court management and administration, we next want to discuss changes that
have been proposed.

Publicity regarding the backload of cases in the federal court
system, the increasing workload per judgeship, and length of time
involved in disposing of cases has found support in Congress. The
support to date has been in the nature of recommending proposals
and introducing bills for congressional action; no legislation has
been passed. In March 1971 the Judicial Conference of the United
States, which is the administrative arm of the federal courts,
recommended that the 92d Congress "establish a Commission whose
function would be to study the present division of the United States
into several judicial circuits and to recommend such changes in the
geographical boundaries of the United States as may be appropriate
for the expeditious and effective disposition of judicial business."[16]

Congress proceeded to pass Public Law 92-489, which created
a 16-member Commission on Revision of the Federal Court Appellate
System, charged to study the existing division of judicial circuits and
to report "its recommendations for changes in the geographical
boundaries of the circuits." The commission, chaired by Senator
Roman Hruska of Nebraska, included members of Congress, judges,
law professors, and practicing lawyers; there were also presidential,
judicial, senatorial, and House appointees. Initial work began in
June 1973 and a report was filed in December of that year. The title

of the report was "The Geographical Boundaries of the Several Judicial Circuits: Recommendations for Change."[17] The specific proposals, which are discussed below, were subsequently introduced in the 93d Congress in September and October 1974 as Senate Bills 2988, 2989, and 2900. Each embodied specific commission recommendations.

The primary recommendation of the Senate bills called for a realignment of the boundaries of the Fifth and Ninth Circuits and an increase in the number of judgeships. The commission had gathered ample statistical evidence on case filings, actions per judgeship, cases pending, cases terminated, and the length of trial before final disposition. For example, the caseload for all 11 circuits had increased more than threefold from 1963 to 1976.[18] In 1963, 69 authorized judgeships were called upon to handle 5,400 cases for an average of 78 per judgeship. By 1976, 97 circuit judgeships were asked to handle 18,408 cases or 190 per judgeship. Problems also were occurring because of the backlog of cases, which in some instances was more than two years. The number of pending cases has more than doubled between 1968 and 1976. Then judge (now Attorney General) Griffin Bell echoed the need for improvements in the judicial machinery, and especially for more judgeships, in his testimony in March 1976 before a House Judiciary Subcommittee. He described the present system as an "antiquated system in which anybody can go to court but nothing happens when they get there."[19] As an example of the backlog, Chief Judge John R. Brown, Fifth Circuit Court of Appeals, Houston, Texas, testified that the non-preference cases brief in September 1976 would not be heard until January 1978, and those briefed in March 1977, not until October 1978. This was assuming no increase in filings.[20] Some circuits, to expedite the disposition of cases, had assigned a district court judge as one member of three-judge panels to decide on cases. This practice did not go without strong objection from a number of members of the trial bar in some states. The Fifth Circuit also had adopted the practice of screening cases, which resulted in almost 60 percent of the cases in 1973 being decided with the parties having a right to oral arguments. Visiting judges were also used to help reduce the caseload; they were district judges, out-of-circuit judges, and senior circuit judges. The problems in caseload and delays were most acute in the Fifth and Ninth Circuits. The commission recommended realignments in their boundaries and increases in circuit judgeships. As we have seen in Table 7.4, these two circuits had the largest number of filings and the heaviest workload per judgeship. Furthermore, these circuits had the largest number of pending cases per judgeship and the largest number of appeals terminated after a hearing or submission. Among these variables, these two circuits had the greatest departure compared to all others.

The district courts as well have suffered from increased workload, with no increases in judgeships since 1970. In 1965 the 341
authorized judgeships handled an average of 304 civil and criminal
cases. The workload estimates for the 399 judgeships in 1976 was
432 cases, nearly 50 percent above 11 years earlier. Nearly 85,000
civil and criminal cases were commenced during the first half of
1976, an increase of 12 percent over the previous year. The entire
1976 civil filings were expected to increase by 130,000 cases and the
criminal cases by 42,200, both all-time high figures.[21] The sharply
rising number of civil cases dealt with social security laws, real
property action, and civil rights. The commission did not discuss
or initiate recommendations that covered district courts; its focus
was on the appellate court system.

The commission indeed recommended a geographic reorganization or realignment of the Fifth and Ninth Circuits. The present
Fifth Circuit would be divided into two circuits, with one retaining
some of the states in the Fifth and the remaining states forming a
new Eleventh Circuit (see Map 7.8). The Ninth Circuit would similarly be divided; the new Ninth Circuit would be reduced in size
geographically and a new Twelfth Circuit would be created (see Map
7.9). The population, caseload, and court business was considered
heavy enough in both the Fifth and Ninth Circuits to more than adequately justify the realignment.

The commission was very concerned about the organization of
any new circuits, urging especially that existing circuit boundaries
be used whenever possible and that there be no one- or two-state
circuits. The reason for not changing existing boundaries of more
than one circuit was to preserve the integrity of the existing organization. The specific language regarding this matter is worthy of
note:

> We have not recommended a general realignment
> of all the circuits. To be sure, the present bound-
> aries are largely the result of historical accident
> and do not satisfy such criteria as parity of case-
> loads and geographical compactness. But these
> boundaries have stood since the nineteenth cen-
> tury, except for the creation of the Tenth Circuit
> in 1929, and whatever the extent of variation in
> the law from circuit to circuit, relocation would
> take from the bench and bar at least some of the
> law familiar to them. Moreover, the commis-
> sion has heard eloquent testimony evidencing the
> sense of community shared by lawyers and judges
> within the present circuits. Except for the most

MAP 7.8: New Fifth and Eleventh Circuit Courts Proposed, 1974

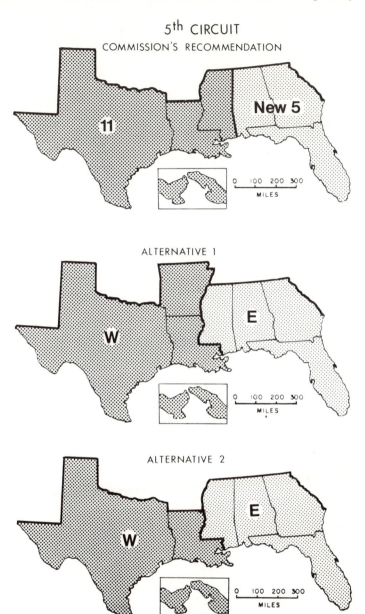

5th CIRCUIT
COMMISSION'S RECOMMENDATION

ALTERNATIVE 1

ALTERNATIVE 2

Source: U.S. Congress, Senate, Committee on the Judiciary,
Subcommittee on Improvements in the Judicial Machinery, Court Re-
alignment: the Realignment of the Fifth and Ninth Circuit Courts of
Appeals, Part I. Hearings on S. 2988, S. 2989, and S. 2900, 93d
Cong., 2d sess., September 24, 25, and 26, October 1, 2, and 3,
1974, pp. 29-31.

MAP 7.9: New Twelfth Circuit Court Proposed, 1974

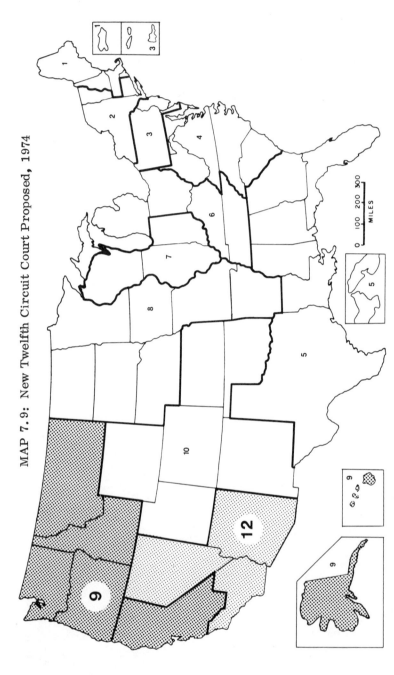

Source: U.S. Congress, Senate, Committee on the Judiciary, Subcommittee on Improvements in the Judicial Machinery, Court Realignment: the Realignment of the Fifth and Ninth Circuit Courts of Appeals, Part 1, Hearings on S. 2988, S. 2989, and S. 2900, 93d Cong., 2d sess., September 24, 25, 26, October 1, 2, 3, 1974, p. 32.

compelling reasons, we are reluctant to disturb
institutions which have acquired not only the respect but also the loyalty of their constituents.[22]

Five criteria were weighed in the reorganization of the Fifth
Circuit. First, circuits should encompass at least three states; no
single-state circuits were to be created. Second, any new circuit
should not require more than nine active judges. Third, inasmuch
as the Courts of Appeals are considered nationwide courts, they
should reflect some diversity in population, socioeconomic interests, and legal business. Fourth, the realignment should follow the
"principle of marginal interference"; that is, excessive interference
with existing boundaries and circuit court structures was deemed undesirable. Finally, no circuit shall contain noncontiguous states.

On the basis of these criteria the commission rejected several
proposals but did offer two alternatives for Fifth Circuit realignment
in its report (Map 7.8). These called for no new circuits being
created but for the formation of an Eastern and a Western Division.
Alternative one would bring Arkansas from the Eighth Circuit and
the Canal Zone into the Western Division, avoiding a two-state circuit. In the second alternative only intracircuit changes would occur;
Texas, Louisiana, and the Canal Zone would form the Western Division, and Florida, Georgia, Alabama, and Mississippi the Eastern
Division. In the recommended and two alternative arrangements,
the number of filings in 1973 would have been roughly equal.

Realignment proposed in the Ninth Circuit was somewhat different than that for the Fifth, primarily because one state, California,
had two-thirds of the caseload in the entire circuit. The commission,
being conscious of the role of circuit courts in the federal system,
adopted the following stands: no single state should constitute a single
federal district; dividing the judicial districts into two circuits would
raise no insoluble or unmanageable problems; and creating two divisions (as offered as alternatives in the Fifth Circuit) would solve the
circuit's problems. In addition to the concern over California, the
areal extent of the circuit in itself almost necessitated realignment;
it stretched from the Arctic Circle to the Mexican border and from
the Rocky Mountains to the Sea of Japan, so that much time was lost
by individual judges traveling. Also the commission felt that the
task of administering the circuit proved difficult with the transport
of records and court exhibits. The time lost simply to accommodate
the organized conferences of judges and to arrange en banc hearings
in itself almost required realignment.

The realignment proposal for the Ninth Circuit set a precedent
in that a state was divided. Commission members deliberated on
how best to reorganize the circuit, mindful that California legitimately

could form a circuit in its own regard. However, the commission
did not favor a single-state circuit because of the possible influence
the state's senators, if elected to long service, could exert on the
court's administration and composition of judges through political
patronage. To avoid the single-state circuit and yet maintain the
necessary degree of judicial mix in the new circuit, the commission
recommended including the Southern and Central Judicial Districts
of California in a new circuit with Arizona and Nevada; California's
Northern and Eastern Judicial Districts would join with the Northwest states to form the new Ninth Circuit. Economic and social
reasons were given as major reasons dividing California; southern
California was recognized to have close economic ties to both neigh-
boring Arizona and Nevada. No alternatives were offered to the
commission's recommendation. This is not to say there was no
opposition to splitting California into two circuits. Among the
major problems envisaged were the possibility of forum shopping,
whereby litigants seeking a hearing in a federal court might ferret
out the circuit in his/her state that would look favorably on the federal law issues. If that developed into a problem Congress could
use such devices as venue restrictions and transfer provisions.
The likelihood that one circuit in California might interpret the law
differently (subtly or substantially) from the other was enough to
raise serious objections to entirely new circuits being defined. Also,
there was the possibility that state agencies might be subject to conflicting orders of federal courts or the problem of parallel lawsuits
occurring simultaneously. The commission felt if these occurred
the Supreme Court could step in and review the cases. The Bar
Association of San Francisco offered five proposals to reorganize
the Ninth Circuit; all favored retaining California as a single state
either by it being a circuit by itself or being included in a circuit of
two or more states.[23] While these were legitimate concerns and
points raised in opposition to the recommendation, the commission
felt that the overriding goal was to provide a realignment that would
make the judicial machinery more effective. No other recommendations were made by the commission even though some attention was
given to the possibility of creating one circuit from five states in
the Northwest (Alaska, Washington, Oregon, Idaho, and Montana)
because of rapid population increases there; but it was felt there
was not sufficient justification for a separate circuit in view of the
1973 statistics.

     After failure to achieve passage of the Senate bills in 1974,
they were reintroduced in the 94th Congress as Senate Bill 729.[24]
Hearings were held in March and May 1975. The new bill, like its
predecessors, was concerned with the reorganization of the Fifth
and Ninth Circuits and an increased number of judgeships in these

circuits. However, this bill had one key feature that was different.
No new circuits were created but administrative divisions were
created within the Fifth and Ninth. Each division would have its own
chief judge, its own circuit executive, and judicial council. The difference between the initial recommendation (which created new circuits) and Senate Bill 729 (which created divisions) was that judges
could be assigned from one division to another without the approval
of the Chief Justice of the United States. Divisions with less than 15
judgeships were preferable to having single circuits with 20 or 30.
Eastern and Western Divisions were created in the Fifth Circuit,
which meant alternative recommendation two was now being adopted
by the commission as a result of further comments and discussion
on the original recommendation. The only change in alternative two
was that the Canal Zone was assigned to the Eastern Division. Northern and Southern Divisions were created in the Ninth Circuit, which
had the same boundaries as in the initial recommendation. California was divided but assurances were taken to guarantee against
sharply conflicting cases being heard simultaneously regarding California law, to prevent excesses in forum shopping, and to prevent
one set of decisions applying to residents in one part of the state and
not to those elsewhere in California. In cases where decisions may
be in conflict or California state law subject to differing interpretation, the chief judge among the two divisions who is senior in service is authorized to convene an en banc hearing. Also a joint committee would be appointed that would strive to achieve relative uniformity in procedures at the local level between districts that hear
appeals.[25]

It is not only Congress that has been active in promoting reforms, but also the American Bar Association's Special Committee
on Coordination of Judicial Improvement, and Chief Justice Burger.
In a series of annual reports on the state of the judiciary, one of his
major pleas has been for more judgeships and realignment. He has
endorsed the proposals for creating divisions in the Ninth and Fifth
Circuits and for additional judgeships.[26] Both measures, he en-
visages, will improve the management of the courts and provide a
smoother delivery of service. In his 1977 address to the American
Bar Association Burger recognized the geographical and administrative problems in court realignment:

> I am well aware that we lawyers and judges,
> addicted as we are to tradition--and sometimes
> sentiment--do not like changes in old patterns,
> but it borders on a "dream world" approach to
> think we can administer justice properly in so
> large an area as the Ninth Circuit under present
> conditions with thirteen appellate judges.[27]

Similar remarks were echoed in support of realignment of the Fifth
Circuit, which stretches from Key West, Florida to the west Texas
border, and, according to Burger, has as many federal judges as
the entire country did when Taft was chief justice; in Taft's day
cries over the mounting administrative problems were also heard.
Burger went on to suggest that other circuits also need constant
monitoring of their caseloads and disposition time. In particular,
the Second Circuit needs watching. Realignment and additional
judgeships are to be monitored as ways to improve the entire judicial machinery, and not to be regarded as tasks that become worthy
of attention only periodically. In this regard Burger stated:

> The only significant change in federal circuits
> made in nearly one half century was to create
> the Tenth Circuit largely out of the Eighth Cir-
> cuit. No comprehensive plan has ever existed
> for the arrangement of the eleven circuits.
> They evolved largely by accident. Like "Topsy,"
> they simply grew. [28]

Alterations to federal court boundaries and the places for circuit court sessions are accomplished by amending the U.S. Code.
The code is the editorial reorganization of the "public, general and
permanent laws of the United States in force."[29] Specific amend-
ments are included in Section 41 of title 28, which deals with the
composition of circuit courts.[30] Other sections deal with places for
sessions, assignments of judges, panels, conferences, venue, and
circuits in which decisions are reviewable. The only new circuit
created in this century has been the Tenth, which was accomplished
by dividing the Eighth in 1929. Prior to that amendment the Circuit
Court of Appeals for the District of Columbia was created in 1922.
The most recent revisions to the code have dealt with increasing the
number of circuit judgeships. In the past 30 years judges have been
added to circuits in 1949, 1954, 1961, 1966, and 1968. There have
not always been additions in the same circuits; the total judgeships
are designed to reflect increases in populations, filings, and caseload per judgeship. The latest (1968) increases were in the Ninth
and Fifth; the Ninth increased its number from nine to 13 and the
Fifth from nine to 15. As has already been stated, concern has
been expressed over having a large number within a single circuit.
Somehow nine has been considered by the commission on revision
as an optimal number; some testimony before the congressional subcommittee questioned the effectiveness of this number.
As of mid-1977 Congress has still failed to pass the omnibus
judgeship bill, now under Senate Bill 11.[31] It has two key features--

the creation of additional judgeships at the district and circuit levels, and a realignment of the Fifth Circuit. Both series of proposals are slightly different from those offered previously.

A total of 107 new judgeships are recommended for the district courts and 25 for the circuit courts. The increased number of judgeships for the districts came as a result of the 1976 quadrennial survey of needs by the Judicial Conference's Committee on Court Administration. Armed with the 1976 data, which showed sharp increases since its 1972 report (when 51 were recommended), the committee was not only concerned with satisfying the present workload, but attempted to project needs through 1980. These 107 would be assigned to 61 districts that previously had a higher-than-average caseload (see Map 7.10). The judicial committee uses filings in excess of 400 per judgeship as a threshold indicator for additional judges. Also there are additional criteria weighed including the complexity of cases, the rates of termination, backlog of pending cases, and the time taken to dispose of cases. The 107 new positions would reduce the sharp variations that now exist between the number of filings per judgeship (Map 7.11) and the judgeship/population ratio (see Map 7.12). In essence the proposed changes should facilitate a streamlining of the judicial machinery at the district level. Failure to pass the bill and allocate these additional judgeships would only further slow judicial services. These proposals will need to be looked at again in the near future as the federal court system is certain to expand. The Federal Judicial Center in March 1971 predicted that there would be 1,129 district court judges needed by 1990, nearly three times the present number.[32]

Senate Bill 11 proposes that there be 25 new circuit judgeships created (see Table 7.5). Most of these would go to the present Fifth and Ninth Circuits. The second key recommendation dealing with the circuits related to realignment. It provides for the Fifth being divided into two circuits, not two divisions as proposed previously. The new Fifth Circuit would include Alabama, Florida, Georgia, Mississippi, and the Canal Zone (see Map 7.13). Texas and Louisiana would be the new Eleventh. The Ninth Circuit realignment, discussed at length and subject to specific proposals in previous bills, was not reorganized in this bill. Instead, the Judicial Council and the Judicial Conference of the United States are to submit recommendations to Congress on ways to efficiently and expeditiously handle the caseload for the circuit. These would be forthcoming once the ten new judges were authorized and the bill became law. Thus the management of the Ninth Circuit's caseload, and in particular, that of California, which requires 13 circuit judges, remains unresolved.

MAP 7.10: Recommended Allocation of 107 New District Court Judgeships

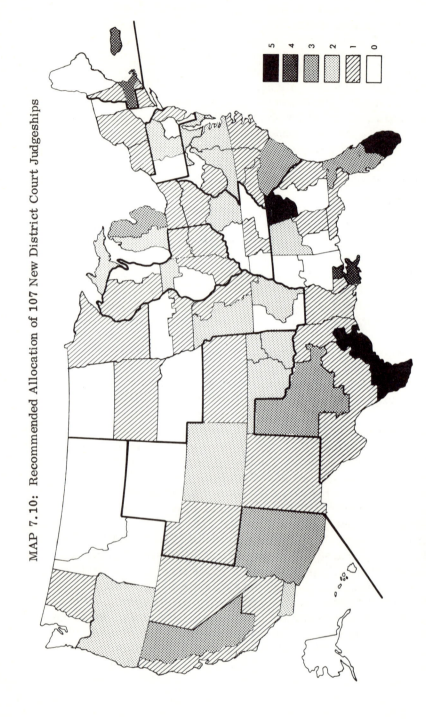

Source: U.S. Congress, Senate, Omnibus Judgeship Bill, Calendar No. 96, Report 95-117, 95th Cong., 1st sess., May 3, 1977, pp. 1-4.

MAP 7.11: Actions per Judgeship with 107 New District Court Judges Recommended, U.S. District Courts, 1976 Data

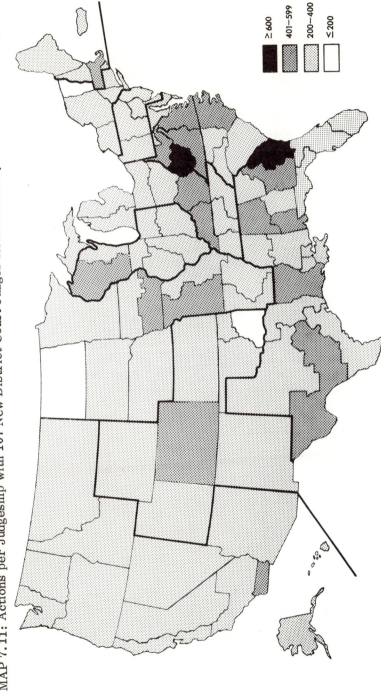

≥600
401–599
200–400
≤200

Sources: U.S. Congress, Senate, Omnibus Judgeship Bill, Calendar No. 96, Report 95–117, 95th Cong., 1st sess., May 3, 1977, pp. 1–4, and Director of the Administrative Office of the U.S. Courts, Management Statistics for United States Courts, 1976 (Washington, D.C.: U.S. Government Printing Office, 1976).

MAP 7.12: Judgeship/Population Ratio with 107 New Judges Appointed, U.S. District Courts, 1970 Population

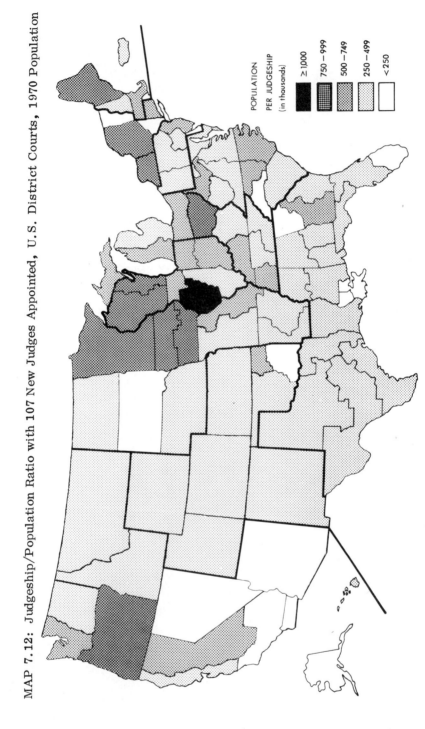

POPULATION
PER JUDGESHIP
(in thousands)

≥ 1,000
750 — 999
500 — 749
250 — 499
< 250

Sources: U.S. Congress, Senate, Omnibus Judgeship Bill, Calendar No. 96, Report 95-117, 95th Cong., 1st sess., May 3, 1977, pp. 1-4, and U.S. Department of Commerce, Bureau of the Census, 1970 Census of Population.

MAP 7.13: Proposed Fifth Circuit Court Realignment, 1977

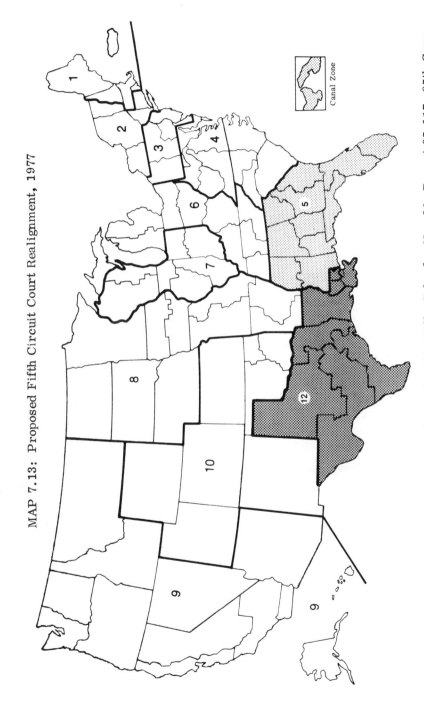

Canal Zone

Source: U.S. Congress, Senate, Omnibus Judgeship Bill, Calendar No. 96, Report 95-117, 95th Cong., 1st sess., May 3, 1977, p. 47.

TABLE 7.5

Recommended Judgeships for Circuit Courts

First Circuit:	1	Seventh Circuit:	1
Second Circuit:	2	Eighth Circuit:	1
Third Circuit:	1	Ninth Circuit:	10
Fourth Circuit:	3	Tenth Circuit:	1
Fifth Circuit:	12	District of Columbia Circuit:	3
Sixth Circuit:	2		

Source: U.S. Congress, Senate, Omnibus Judgeship Bill, Calendar No. 96, Report No. 95-117, 95th Cong., 1st sess., May 3, 1977, p. 16.

The reorganization of the present Fifth was justified on the grounds of the increased caseload, delays in disposing of cases, and a large volume of cases pending. The geographical queries mainly centered on what states to include in the new Fifth and Eleventh Circuits. Earlier proposals centered on where to place Arkansas, Mississippi, and the Canal Zone; all three in previous recommendations had been assigned the new Eleventh or a Western Division. State bar associations in Arkansas and Mississippi expressed their views on the proposals. The State Bar of Arkansas did not wish to be dislocated from the Eighth Circuit, to which it has been attached for many years; it said it "is more akin to the laws of states in the Eighth Circuit than to the laws of Louisiana and Texas," which have a civil law derived from the Napoleonic code.[33] Mississippi preferred to remain with Alabama and Georgia as it has historical antecedents with Georgia Territory and did not wish to be tied to civil law states (Texas and Louisiana). The Canal Zone was considered appropriately tied to the Fifth as it has direct airline connections with Miami, not New Orleans. In the proposed bill the Fifth and Eleventh Circuits would have 14 and 12 judgeships, respectively, and 140 and 139 filings per judgeship, using 1976 data. The total caseload would be 1,961 for the Fifth and 1,668 for the Eleventh when 1976 data are considered.[34]

SUMMARY

The questions of court administration and organization are discussed at length in this chapter. That organization is examined from a geographical perspective; namely, how the geographer looks at the administration and organization of space, and how specific court statistics can be used to illustrate cartographically variations within states, between states, and between regions. A number of measures are mapped and discussed in an effort to demonstrate the nature of reforms needed in court administration. Specific proposals for recommendation are advanced by demonstrating cartographically and statistically the efficiency that will result if they are incorporated. The congressional hearings and bills proposed have identified the two most critical problems facing the system, that of realignment of the circuit courts and the allocation of new judgeships in both the circuits and the districts. If the proposed legislation is approved, and it has the backing of the chief justice, various state bar associations, scholars, and lawyers, it will go a long way toward correcting the present administrative problems. The reforms will not only streamline the operation of the judicial machinery, but will demonstrate to the public the legal profession's and congressional members' desire to see that the system operates smoothly, efficiently, and with equity.

NOTES

1. Some useful references on the organizational aspects of courts are Walter F. Murphy and G. Herman Pritchett, Courts, Judges, and Politics: An Introduction to the Judicial Process (New York: Random House, 1961), pp. 33-64; Herbert Jacob, Justice in America (Boston: Little, Brown, 1964), pp. 131-48; Ernest C. Friesen et al., Managing the Courts (Indianapolis: Bobbs-Merrill, 1971); Seldon Goldman and Thomas P. Jahnige, The Federal Courts as a Political System (New York: Harper and Row, 1971), pp. 22-33; and Richard J. Richardson and Kenneth N. Vines, The Politics of Federal Courts: Lower Courts in the United States (Boston: Little, Brown, 1970).

2. Lesley Oelsner, "Burger Scores Congress for Inaction on Judges," New York Times, February 24, 1975, p. 14; Warren Weaver, Jr., "Burger Calls Congress Remiss on Need for More Judgeships," New York Times, January 4, 1976, pp. 1, 42; and "Chief Justice Burger's 1977 Report to the ABA," American Bar Association Journal 63 (1977): 504-09.

3. Henry Robert Glick, "The System of State and Local Courts," Current History 60 (1971): 346.

4. Ibid., p. 347.

5. Ibid. Glick cites Survey of Judicial System of Maryland (New York: Institute of Judicial Administration, 1967), pp. 11-12.

The geographic variations at local levels are illustrated in L. M. Friedman and R. V. Percival, "A Tale of Two Counties: Litigation in Alameda and San Benito Counties," Law and Society 10 (1976): 267-302.

6. See the following for administrative court reforms at the state level: James E. Farmer, "Indiana Modernizes Its Courts," Judicature 54 (1971): 327-30; Joe R. Greenhill and John W. Quinn, "Judicial Reform of Our Texas Courts--A Reexamination of Three Important Aspects," Baylor Law Review 23 (1971): 204-26; Ralph N. Kleps, "State Court Modernization in the 1970's: Forces for Reform in California," Judicature 55 (1972): 292-97; "State Court Progress at a Glance," Judicature 56 (1973): 427-30; and Larry L. Berg et al., "The Consequences of Judicial Reform: A Comparative Analysis of the California and Iowa Appellate System," Western Political Quarterly 28 (1975): 263-80. Court reform in general is treated by Carl Baar, "Reorganization of the Federal Judicial System," Judicature 55 (1972): 282-87; Carl McGowan, "Toward Better Organization," American Bar Association Journal 59 (1973): 1267-1270; Mark W. Cannon, "The Federal Judicial System: Highlights of Administrative Modernization," Criminology 12 (1974): 10-24; and "Symposium on Judicial Administration in the United States," Arizona State Law Journal, no. 4 (1974): 519-72.

7. Barbara Schulert and Bill Hoelzel, "Court Reform, the Unheralded Winner of the 1976 Elections," Judicature 60 (1977): 281-89.

8. The following four documents are most useful in ferreting out the rationale, justification, and recommendations that went into the various bills introduced in recent years. U.S. Congress, Senate, Committee on the Judiciary, Subcommittee on Improvements in the Judicial Machinery, Court Realignment: The Realignment of the Fifth and Ninth Circuit Courts of Appeals, Part 1, Hearings on S. 2988, S. 2989, and S. 2900, 93d Cong., 2d sess., September 24, 25, 26, October 1, 2, 3, 1974 (hereafter cited as Circuit Realignment, 1974); U.S. Congress, Senate, Committee on the Judiciary, Subcommittee on Improvements in the Judicial Machinery, Court Realignment: The Realignment of the Fifth and Ninth Circuit Courts of Appeals, Part 2, Hearings on S. 729, 94th Cong., 1st sess., March 18, 19, May 20, 21, 1975 (hereafter cited as Circuit Realignment, 1975); U.S. Congress, Senate, Reorganization of the Ninth Judicial Circuit, Calendar No. 1163, Report No. 94-1227, 94th Cong., 2d sess., September 9, 1976; and U.S. Congress, Senate, Omnibus Judgeship Bill, Calendar No. 96, Report No. 95-117, 95th Cong., 1st sess., May 3, 1977.

9. See the various remarks and accounts regarding Chief Justice Burger's annual message on the state of the judiciary, cited in Note 2.

10. The geographical perspective on organizing space is discussed in John A. Jakle, Stanley D. Brunn, and Curtis C. Roseman, Human Spatial Behavior: A Social Geography (North Scituate, Mass.: Duxbury Press, 1976), pp. 245-75. The study of social science inputs into the judicial field is welcomed in James B. McMillan, "Social Science and the District Court: the Observation of a Journeyman Trial Judge," Law and Contemporary Problems 39 (1975): 157-63. He states in conclusion: "Social science is entitled to a respected place in the halls of justice. The study of peoples and their problems is a natural prerequisite of the legal decision of problems among people."

11. Boundaries and their evolution and impact on human behavior are treated in Stanley D. Brunn, Geography and Politics in America (New York: Harper and Row, 1974), pp. 177-96.

12. Director of the Administrative Office of the U.S. Courts, Management Statistics for United States Courts (Washington, D.C.: U.S. Government Printing Office, October 1976).

13. Erwin C. Surrency, "A History of Federal Courts," Missouri Law Review 28 (1963): 224-36. See also the references on court organization cited in Note 1.

14. Peter Graham Fish, The Politics of Federal Judicial Administration (Princeton: Princeton University Press, 1973), p. 4. His general discussion on the political and geographical developments in the nation's federal court system (pp. 1-39) is succinct and well documented.

15. In some cases the location of courthouses and the allocation of judges was more of a hit-and-miss process than one following a uniform pattern. The rivalry between sections of a state and newly settled towns was frequent. See the Iowa case presented and debated in Congressional Record, 46th Cong., 2d sess., 1880, vol. 10, pt. 4, pp. 3443-3446. Fish, op. cit., p. 12, cites a congressman in 1872 as saying: "The first proposition is to build a new place of holding court, the next is to create a new district with a district judge, marshal, and attorney; the next step is to build a courthouse-post office; and if this system has to go on . . . we shall have in the United States as many places of holding courts as there are counties, and instead of having sixty or seventy district judges you will have six or seven hundred."

16. U.S. Congress, Senate, Reorganization of Ninth Judicial Circuit, op. cit., p. 9.

17. Commission on Revision of Federal Court Appellate System, The Geographical Boundaries of the Several Judicial Circuits: Recommendations for Change (Washington, D.C.: U.S. Government Printing Office, 1973). This report is included in Circuit Realignment, 1974, pp. 20-63.

18. Director of the Administrative Office of the U.S. Courts, op. cit. Two recent studies that have examined in detail the federal courts, using masses of data, are J. Woodford Howard, Jr., "Litigation Flows in Three United States Courts of Appeal," Law and Society 8 (1973): 33-54, and Joel Grossman and Austin Sarat, "Litigation in the Federal Courts: A Comparative Perspective," Law and Society 9 (1975): 321-46.

19. Quoted in "Editorial Opinion and Comment," American Bar Association Journal 63 (April 1977): 55.

20. From table cited in testimony, in Circuit Realignment, 1975, op. cit., p. 40.

21. Administrative Office of the United States Courts, Semiannual Report of the Director, 1976 (Washington, D.C.: 1976), p. 9.

22. Circuit Realignment, 1974, op. cit., p. 26.

23. The Bar Association of San Francisco's report on the revisions of the Ninth Circuit are included in Circuit Realignment, 1974, op. cit., pp. 299-319; their recommendations on the organization of states are on page 308.

24. Circuit Realignment, 1975, op. cit.

25. U.S. Congress, Senate, Reorganization of the Ninth Judicial Circuit, op. cit.

26. Ibid.

27. "Chief Justice Burger's 1977 Report to the ABA," op. cit., p. 507.

28. Ibid., p. 508.

29. Joe Morehead, Introduction to United States Public Documents (Littleton, Colo.: Libraries Unlimited, 1975), p. 110.

30. U.S. Statutes at Large, 61st Cong., 3d sess., Chapter 5, pp. 1105-1130, contains the counties identified in each court district. This Senate Bill 7031 to "codify, revise, and amend the laws relating to the judiciary" was passed March 3, 1911 and became Public Law 475. Other chapters of this statute define the organization of courts, their jurisdiction, removal of cases, and circuit courts of appeal. Congressional discussion on S. 7031 is also interesting reading. See especially U.S. Congress, Senate, Congressional Record, 61st Cong., 3d sess., January 16, 1911, vol. 46, part 1, pp. 928-54, January 27, 1911, pp. 1536-1545, and February 8, 1911, pp. 2131-2140, for the Senate discussion. The House Resolution 23377 is contained in U.S. Congress, House, Congressional Record, 61st Cong., 3d sess., vol. 46, Pt. 4, February 23, 1911, pp. 3216-3220 and March 2, 1911, pp. 3998-4012.

31. U.S. Congress, Senate, Omnibus Judgeship Bill, op. cit.

32. Ibid., p. 8.

33. Ibid., p. 45.

34. Ibid., p. 47.

ABOUT THE AUTHORS

KEITH D. HARRIES is Professor of Geography at Oklahoma State University. His research has been reported in various journals, including Criminology, Social Indicators Research, the Annals of the Association of American Geographers, and the Professional Geographer. One previous book, The Geography of Crime and Justice, appeared in 1974. Harries was an undergraduate at the London School of Economics; his graduate degrees are from UCLA.

STANLEY D. BRUNN, Professor of Geography at Michigan State University, has research interests in social and political geography, urban geography, and the geography of the future. He has published articles on a variety of topics, including black migration, poverty, elections, government spending, jury selection, jurisdictional geography, political reorganization and futures. His book Geography and Politics in America appeared in 1974, and he was co-author of Human Spatial Behavior: A Social Geography (1976). Brunn has an M.A. from the University of Wisconsin and a Ph.D from Ohio State University.

RELATED TITLES
Published by
Praeger Special Studies

BARGAINING FOR JUSTICE: Case Disposition
and Reform in the Criminal Courts
>
> Suzann R. Thomas Buckle
>
> Leonard G. Buckle

CRIMINAL RECIDIVISM IN NEW YORK CITY: An
Evaluation of the Impact of Rehabilitation and
Diversion Services
>
> Robert Fishman

TOWARD A JUST AND EFFECTIVE SENTENCING
SYSTEM: Agenda for Legislative Reform
>
> Pierce O'Donnell
>
> Michael J. Churgin
>
> Dennis E. Curtis

VICTIMS, CRIME, AND SOCIAL CONTROL
>
> Eduard A. Ziegenhagen